BBC
DOCTOR WHO
THE OFFICIAL
COOKBOOK

BBC DOCTOR WHO

THE OFFICIAL COOKBOOK

JOANNA FARROW

PHOTOGRAPHY AND PROP STYLING
HAARALA HAMILTON

HARPER DESIGN
An Imprint of HarperCollins Publishers

CONTENTS

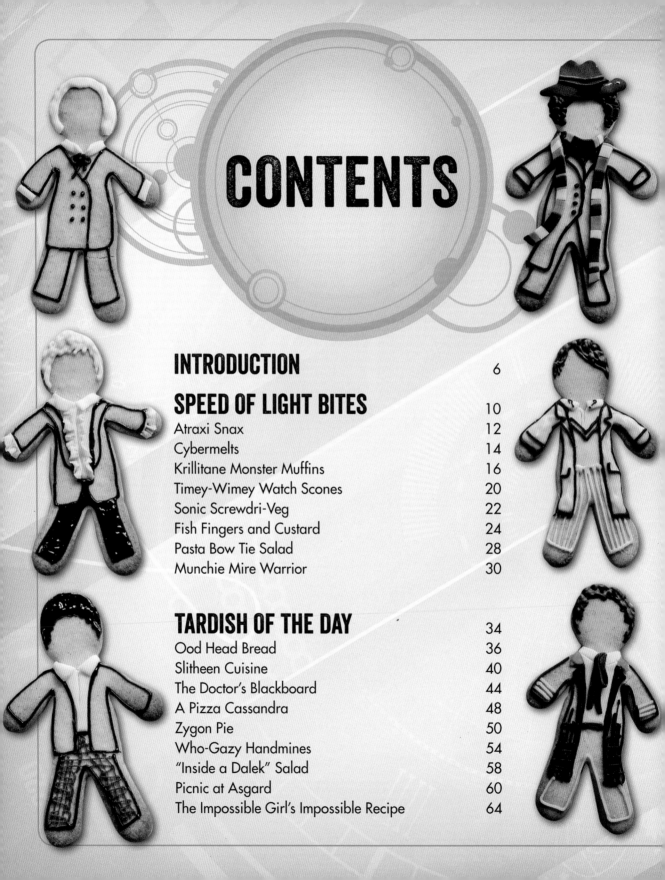

INTRODUCTION

How much the Doctor, or any Time Lord, actually needs to eat has never really been established. We know he likes jelly babies, and fish fingers and custard. He enjoys Sergeant Benton's coffee too, as well as good cheese and fine wine. But whether he really needs to eat and drink, or just enjoys the taste, is a mystery.

But whatever the truth, there is certainly plenty of food and drink in *Doctor Who*. And there's plenty of opportunity to turn some of the elements that have made *Doctor Who* so successful over the years into food and drink, too.

Doctor Who: The Official Cookbook is an inspiring collection of recipes, from simple snacks and teatime treats to spectacular centerpiece cakes. All things Whovian are included, from the Doctor's favorite foods (yes, there are some, whether he actually needs them or not), to the TARDIS and some iconic Who settings.

And of course, what *Doctor Who* cookbook would be complete without the monsters? Many of the Doctor's enemies don't need food—although some do like to feast on human flesh. The Cybermen simply reenergize themselves, while the Sontarans absorb pure energy through the probic vent on the back of their neck. The Zygons drink the milk of their Skarasen creatures, like the Loch Ness Monster. How—or if—the Daleks ingest is a mystery although we know they need static electricity … But what they all have in common is that—with the help of these recipes—each one can be made to taste so much better than they look!

You'll need little excuse to cook from your *Doctor Who* recipes. You might be looking for something fun and a bit different for a family supper, or simply fancy some tasty treats to nibble on as you watch the latest episode. Or why not push the TARDIS out and have a themed party?

The recipes vary considerably in their complexity. Some are easy enough for the kids and little Time Lords to help cook, like Fish fingers and Custard, Timey-Wimey Watch Scones, or Banana Party Pops. There's even the whole set of Doctors in the form of little iced cookies. Hours of fun to be had decorating those! Others, like the Extermi-Cake and Sweet Silence require more patience and commitment, but even these are perfectly approachable.

Just make sure you have all the right ingredients for decoration. Allow time for cakes to cool before cutting them to shape and for the icing, where necessary, to set. Even if your finished result isn't quite cookbook perfect, it'll still look really impressive and set the scene for a memorable Whovian feast.

All you need to do then is invite a few Time Lords round and tuck in!

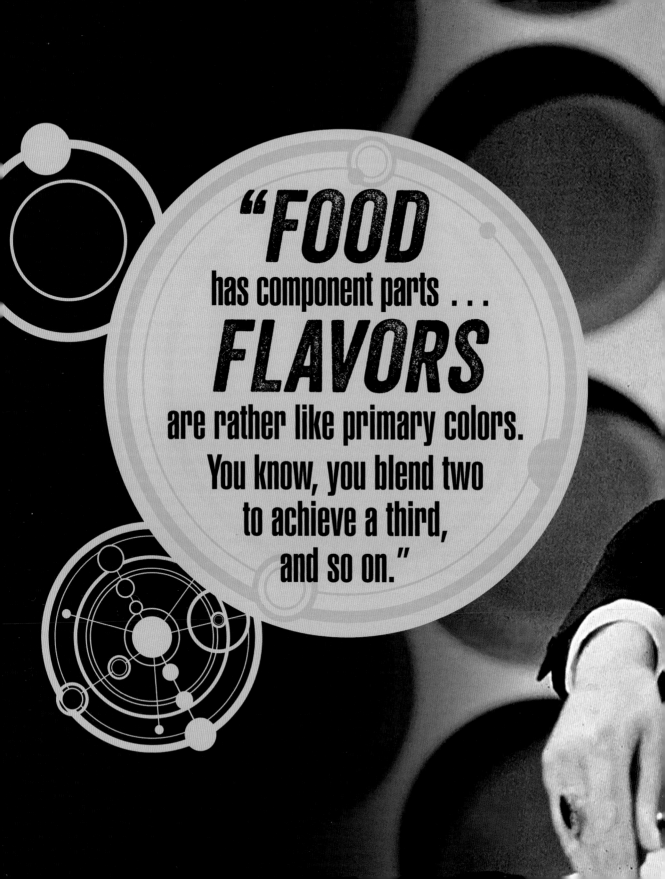

"**FOOD**
has component parts . . .
FLAVORS
are rather like primary colors.
You know, you blend two
to achieve a third,
and so on."

SPEED OF LIGHT BITES

ATRAXI SNAX

If Prisoner Zero—or any other prisoner come to that—escapes through a crack in time, then these are just the things to snack on while you hunt him down and threaten to destroy whole worlds. Breadsticks, homemade cheesy cookies, and hard-boiled eggs make up these tasty treats, perfect for a party snack or to share in the cabin of your pursuit ship. You could even try a mini version for smaller appetites using quails' eggs and wholewheat stick snacks. A bowl of spicy mayonnaise for dipping wouldn't go amiss either!

MAKES 8 SNACKS

¾ cup all-purpose flour
⅓ cup firm unsalted butter, cut into
    small pieces
1 medium egg yolk
1 packed cup Cheddar, grated,
    plus 3 tbsp
a little beaten egg white
4-oz pack of thin breadsticks
4 medium eggs, hard-boiled
    and shelled
4 blueberries
blue food coloring powder

YOU WILL NEED:
a fine paintbrush

1 Preheat the oven to 400°F. Line two baking sheets with baking parchment.

2 Put the flour in a food processor and add the butter. Process until the mixture resembles coarse breadcrumbs. Add the egg yolk and 1 packed cup cheese and process to a smooth dough. Turn out onto the counter and cut in half. Chill or freeze half the dough for making little savory cookies another time (you only need half for this recipe). Shape the dough into a thick, short log, 5 inches long.

3 Cut the dough into eight slices and space the slices well apart on the baking sheets. Brush with beaten egg white.

4 Break the breadsticks into varying lengths and press around the edges of each circle of dough. Make sure you press the ends in firmly so they'll be held in place as the dough cooks. Bake for 10 minutes until the dough is pale golden. Sprinkle the centers with the remaining 3 tbsp cheese and return to the oven for another 2 minutes to melt the cheese.

5 While cooking, cut the ends off the hard-boiled eggs (this will leave a slice of about ¼ inch in the center to use up in a salad or sandwich). Press an end of egg onto each cookie while the cheese is still soft. Let cool.

6 Using a small teaspoon or the tip of a small sharp knife, make a small dip in the top of each egg. Halve the blueberries and place a half, cut-side face up, in each scooped out egg. Use a fine, dry paintbrush to paint the blue powder onto the breadsticks.

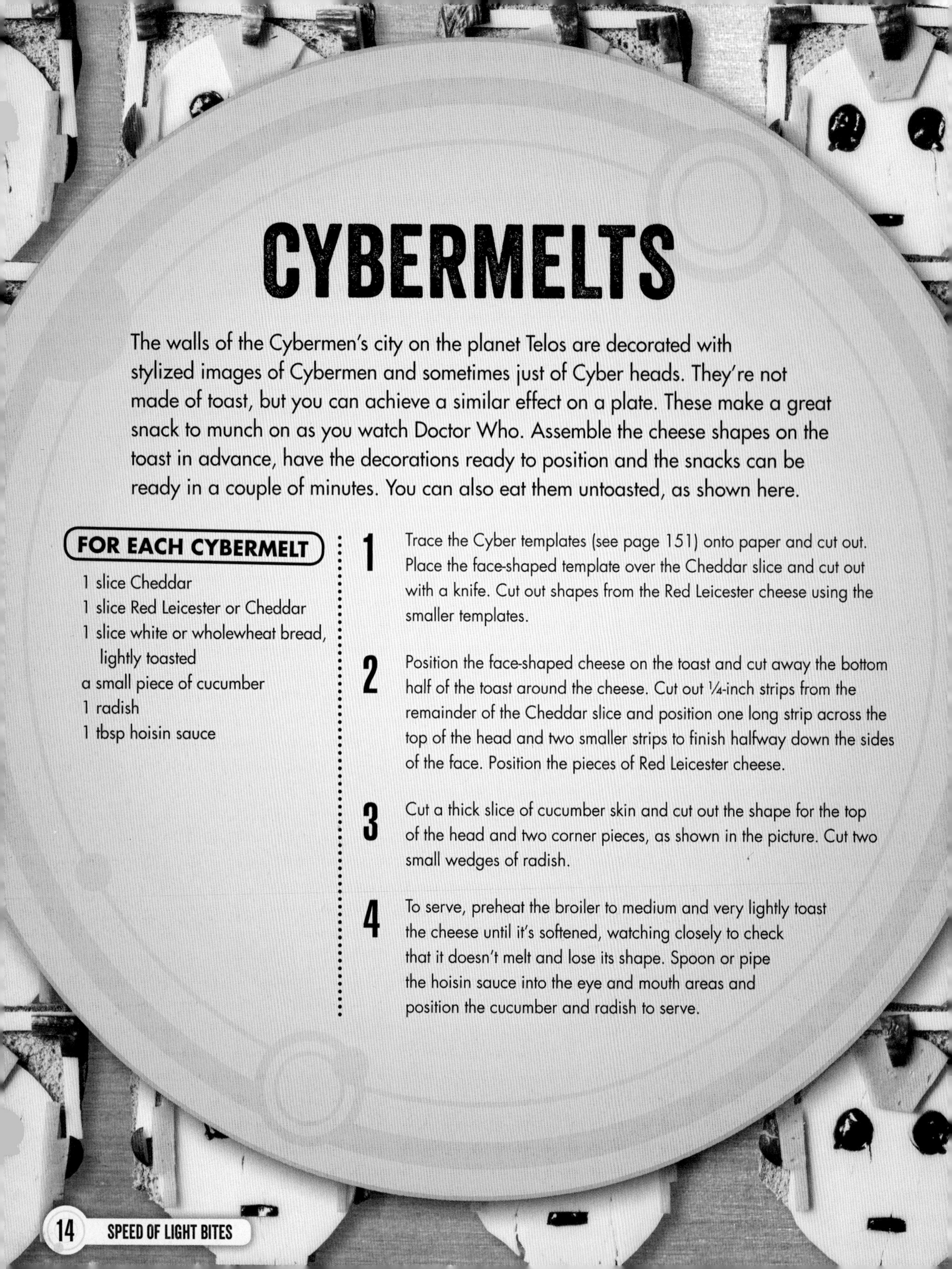

CYBERMELTS

The walls of the Cybermen's city on the planet Telos are decorated with stylized images of Cybermen and sometimes just of Cyber heads. They're not made of toast, but you can achieve a similar effect on a plate. These make a great snack to munch on as you watch Doctor Who. Assemble the cheese shapes on the toast in advance, have the decorations ready to position and the snacks can be ready in a couple of minutes. You can also eat them untoasted, as shown here.

FOR EACH CYBERMELT

1 slice Cheddar
1 slice Red Leicester or Cheddar
1 slice white or wholewheat bread,
   lightly toasted
a small piece of cucumber
1 radish
1 tbsp hoisin sauce

1 Trace the Cyber templates (see page 151) onto paper and cut out. Place the face-shaped template over the Cheddar slice and cut out with a knife. Cut out shapes from the Red Leicester cheese using the smaller templates.

2 Position the face-shaped cheese on the toast and cut away the bottom half of the toast around the cheese. Cut out ¼-inch strips from the remainder of the Cheddar slice and position one long strip across the top of the head and two smaller strips to finish halfway down the sides of the face. Position the pieces of Red Leicester cheese.

3 Cut a thick slice of cucumber skin and cut out the shape for the top of the head and two corner pieces, as shown in the picture. Cut two small wedges of radish.

4 To serve, preheat the broiler to medium and very lightly toast the cheese until it's softened, watching closely to check that it doesn't melt and lose its shape. Spoon or pipe the hoisin sauce into the eye and mouth areas and position the cucumber and radish to serve.

KRILLITANE MONSTER MUFFINS

The Krillitanes are a composite species who absorb the characteristics and bits of the physical appearance of the races they conquer. So we can't be exactly sure what they look like at any given time … That also means that if your Krillitane doesn't look quite like the Krillitanes the Doctor encountered, then don't worry. It could still be a Krillitane. This savory treat is made using two muffin sizes, assembled into one big Krillitane monster, perfect for a party so everyone can take whichever size muffin they fancy, or have room for. Kids would enjoy both the baking and decorating, so here's your chance to leave them to it.

MAKES 9 LARGE MUFFINS AND 11 MINI MUFFINS

scant 1½ cups frozen corn
3½ oz lean bacon, diced
1⅓ cups self-rising flour
1 cup cornmeal
2 tsp baking powder
4 tbsp chopped cilantro
2 medium eggs
scant 1 cup milk
5 tbsp mild olive oil or sunflower oil

TO FINISH:

scant 1 cup smooth peanut butter
3 oz ready-salted potato chips (about 3 small bags)
4-oz package of thin breadsticks
1 small red onion
1 cherry tomato
1 slice of Cheddar
6 savory crackers

YOU WILL NEED:

a 12-cup muffin tray with 3-inch wide and 1¼-inch deep paper liners, a 12-cup mini muffin tray with 1¾-inch wide and ¾-inch deep paper liners, and a small paper pastry bag or a plastic food bag

1 Preheat the oven to 400°F. Line 9 sections of a muffin tray with paper muffin liners. Line 11 sections of a mini muffin tray with mini muffin liners.

2 Cook the corn in boiling water for 2 minutes, then drain. Heat a frying pan and fry the bacon for 5 minutes, stirring frequently, until golden.

3 Combine the flour, cornmeal, baking powder, and cilantro in a bowl. Stir in the corn and bacon. Beat together the eggs, milk, and oil and add to the bowl. Stir lightly until the ingredients are only just combined. Spoon into the paper liners, filling them almost full. Bake the smaller muffins for 10 minutes and the larger ones for 15 minutes. Let cool.

CONTINUES ON NEXT PAGE ▶

SPEED OF LIGHT BITES

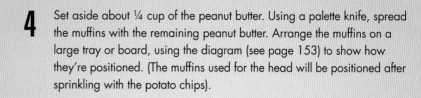

4 Set aside about ¼ cup of the peanut butter. Using a palette knife, spread the muffins with the remaining peanut butter. Arrange the muffins on a large tray or board, using the diagram (see page 153) to show how they're positioned. (The muffins used for the head will be positioned after sprinkling with the potato chips).

5 Half open the bags of potato chips but leave the chips inside. Crush the bags in your hands to crumble them as finely as you can. Sprinkle the potato chips all over the muffins, filling the gaps between them. Press the breadsticks onto the limbs, hands, and feet as shown. Cut small pieces of red onion and position on the hands and feet for claws. Rest the two "head" muffins in position.

6 Put the remaining peanut butter in a small paper pastry bag or into one corner of a plastic food bag. Snip off a small tip. Pipe the outlines of the eyes and nostrils onto the head and sprinkle with a few more chip crumbs. Cut small pieces of red onion and push into the eyes and nostrils. Add even smaller pieces of tomato for the centers of the eyes. Cut small ears and teeth from the cheese and press into the peanut butter. Position the crackers to represent wings.

"What you see is a simple morphic illusion. Scratch the surface and the *TRUE KRILLITANE* lies beneath."

TIMEY-WIMEY WATCH SCONES

Both the Doctor and the Master have hidden their true essence and pretended to be human. It was such a good disguise even they didn't know who they really were! Both of them kept their real selves locked away inside a pocket watch. You probably can't keep a Time Lord's soul inside these scones, but they certainly look the part. The secret of most scone recipes is to roll the dough out thickly so the scones rise up during baking. This recipe is an exception to the rule as the dough should be rolled fairly thin for shaping the watch. Cook them briefly though or they'll overbake to a cookie!

MAKES 7 SCONES

about 1¾ cups self-rising flour, plus extra for dusting

1 tsp baking powder

4¾ tbsp firm butter, cut into small pieces

½ packed cup Cheddar, finely grated

⅔–¾ cup milk

5 tbsp brown sauce

1½ tsp ground paprika

14 slices of Gouda

1 small carrot

½ small green bell pepper, seeded

3½ oz cheese-flavored potato hoops

YOU WILL NEED:

an 3-inch and a 2¾-inch plain round cutter, a paper pastry bag, or plastic food bag, and a piping tip or small cutter

1 Preheat the oven to 425°F. Grease a large baking sheet. Put the flour and baking powder into a food processor and add the butter. Process until the mixture resembles fine breadcrumbs. Briefly process in the grated cheese. Add ⅔ cup of the milk and blend until the mixture comes together to form a soft dough, adding the remaining milk if the dough is dry.

2 Tip out onto a floured counter and roll out to a ½ inch thickness. Cut out circles using a 3-inch plain cutter. Roll out the dough trimmings to ¼-inch thickness and cut out seven winders. Cut deep grooves into these and press against the sides of the scones, securing in place with a little milk. Bake for about 8 minutes until risen and turning pale golden. Transfer to a wire rack to cool.

3 Carefully slice the top off each scone and set aside. Blend 3 tbsp of the brown sauce with the paprika and put in a paper pastry bag or spoon into one corner of a plastic food bag. Twist the open end to secure and snip off the smallest tip you can so the sauce can be piped in a fine line.

4 Spread a little of the remaining brown sauce onto the cut side of each scone half. Cut out a 2¾-inch circle from each of the cheese slices. Position one on each half of the scones to make watch bases and watch lids.

5 Cut very thin slices of carrot and cut out small circles using the end of a piping tip or small cutter. Arrange two on each watch base. Pipe numerals onto each watch face and a border around the edges of the cheese circles using the pastry bag. Cut fine shreds of green bell pepper and position for the watch hands.

6 Snap the potato hoops in half. Position one piece against each winder and interlock the remainder together to create a watch chain effect.

SONIC SCREWDRI-VEG

The Doctor's trusty Sonic Screwdriver has got him out of a lot of tight spots. He's used it to open locked doors, to explode landmines, even occasionally to undo screws. But he's never actually had to eat it. At least, not so far … Serve healthy vegetables in a fun way with these Sonic Screwdriver-shaped veggie kebabs. Lightly cooked with a little garlic butter, they're good on their own or with a meaty meal.

MAKES 4 KEBABS

1 slender carrot
4 slender zucchini, at least
  4¼ inches long
4 medium mushrooms
2 tbsp butter
1 small garlic clove, crushed
4 large pitted black olives, halved
8 frozen baby fava beans, thawed
  and skinned
salt and freshly ground black
  pepper

YOU WILL NEED:
4 bamboo skewers

1 Peel the carrot, cut into four chunks, and cook in boiling water for 5 minutes to soften. Add the zucchini and cook for 1 minute. Drain and cool slightly.

2 Peel two zucchini and cut into four 2-inch lengths. Make deep, lengthwise grooves into the remaining zucchini (so they look stripy), and cut into four 2-inch lengths. Cut four ¾-inch lengths and eight ¼-inch lengths from the carrots. Taper the thicker lengths at the ends. Cut four deep wedges out of each mushroom so you end up with a four-pronged shape. Cut four bamboo skewers down to 7-inch lengths.

3 Line a broiler pan with foil. Melt the butter and mix with the garlic and a little seasoning.

4 Thread each skewer as follows, pushing the vegetables down to the ends of the skewer:
thick piece of carrot, tapered end first
peeled length of zucchini
thin piece of carrot
two olive halves, rounded ends touching
thin piece of carrot
striped length of zucchini
mushroom, rounded-end first

5 Preheat the broiler to medium. Place the kebabs on the broiler rack and brush with the garlic butter. Grill for 3–5 minutes, turning once until slightly softened. Thread two fava beans onto the tip of each skewer and serve hot.

FISH FINGERS AND CUSTARD

Doctor Who tucked into the weird combination of frozen fish fingers and ready-made custard. Thankfully in this recipe, a rich cheese sauce takes the place of custard for dipping your delicious homemade fish fingers.

SERVES 4

14-oz piece skinned and boned
  cod or haddock fillet
1 tbsp all-purpose flour
1 medium egg, beaten
1¼ cups fresh breadcrumbs
oil, for shallow-frying

FOR THE "CUSTARD":
1 tbsp butter
1¾ tbsp all-purpose flour
1¼ cups milk
1 tsp Dijon mustard
scant 1 packed cup sharp
  Cheddar, grated
good pinch of ground turmeric
salt and freshly ground black
  pepper

1 Cut the fish across into ¾-inch wide fingers. Put the flour on a plate and season with a little salt and pepper. Put the egg on another plate and the breadcrumbs on a third. Dust the fish in the flour, then coat in beaten egg and finally in the breadcrumbs.

2 For the custard, melt the butter in a small pan. Add the flour and cook over a gentle heat, stirring for 1 minute. Remove from the heat and gradually blend in the milk, whisking until smooth. Return to a gentle heat and cook, stirring continuously, until the sauce is thickened and smooth. Add the mustard, cheese, and turmeric and cook for another 2 minutes. Remove from the heat.

3 Heat a ½-inch depth of oil in a frying pan. Once hot enough (a sprinkling of breadcrumbs should sizzle when added to the pan), cook half the fish fingers for 4–5 minutes, turning once until golden. Drain on a plate lined with paper towels and keep warm while you cook the remainder.

4 Reheat the cheese sauce gently and serve with the fish fingers.

PASTA BOW TIE SALAD

As bow ties were the Eleventh Doctor's favorite accessory, this would surely be his favorite salad! And if you happen to have a spare Fez about the place that you can serve it in, then so much the better. The salad can be served warm or cold as a light meal on its own or as an accompaniment to chicken, pork, or salmon.

SERVES 4–5

2 red bell peppers, seeded and cut into small pieces
2 green bell peppers, seeded and cut into small pieces
5 tbsp olive oil
3½ oz chorizo sausage, skinned and cut into small dice
2 tbsp pine nuts
7 oz dried pasta bows
2 tbsp capers, drained
1 tbsp basil leaves, torn into pieces
a squeeze of lemon juice
salt

1 Preheat the oven to 400°F. Sprinkle the peppers in a roasting pan and drizzle with 2 tbsp of the oil. Bake for 30 minutes. Add the chorizo and pine nuts and bake for another 30 minutes until the peppers are lightly browned.

2 Meanwhile, cook the pasta in a pan of plenty of boiling, lightly salted water for 12–15 minutes until tender. Drain and transfer to a bowl.

3 If serving warm, stir the baked peppers, pine nuts, and chorizo, capers, basil, lemon juice, and remaining oil into the pasta. Stir well to combine. If serving cold, let the pasta cool before stirring in the remaining ingredients.

"Bow ties ARE COOL"

MUNCHIE MIRE WARRIOR

Although Odin's formidable looking Mire warriors appear tricky to make, they're actually not as hard to create as they are to fight off if they attack your village. You can shape and bake the warrior in advance and reheat it, covered with foil, to freshen it up. It also freezes well.

MAKES 1 BREAD

2 cups wholewheat flour

2 cups + 3 tbsp self-rising white flour, plus extra for dusting

½ tsp baking soda

1 tsp salt

4 tbsp olive oil

scant 1¼ cups buttermilk

2–4 tbsp milk

2 thin breadsticks

1 tbsp HP sauce or Hoisin sauce

1 Preheat the oven to 400°F. Grease a large baking sheet. Put the flours, baking soda, salt, and olive oil in a bowl. Add the buttermilk and 2 tbsp of the regular milk and mix to a dough with a round-bladed knife. Add the remaining milk if the dough feels dry. Turn out onto the counter and knead into a smooth ball.

2 Take 5 oz of the dough and shape into a flat cone shape. Place on the center of the baking sheet with the thin end toward you for the body. Take 8 oz dough and shape into a thick wedge (like a wedge of cheese). Position for the head so the thin end rests over the body. Shape two 3-oz sausage shapes and press into position either side of the body so the shoulders come almost halfway up the sides of the head. Shape another 2-oz sausage of dough and add to the end of the monster's left arm. Add a ¾-oz piece of dough to the end of the other arm. For the right hand, take a ¾-oz ball of dough and cut slits into one side with a knife. Pinch out into claws and press into position.

CONTINUES ON NEXT PAGE ▶

3 Shape two 1½-oz sausage shapes of dough and position for the tops of the legs. Add ½-oz pieces to the ends for the lower legs and small pieces for the feet. Push two lengths of breadstick into the monster's left arm to resemble the gun. Press deep diagonal grooves into the trunk of the body to define the ribs.

4 Thinly roll out the remaining dough on a lightly floured counter. From this cut out all the armor pieces as shown in the picture and position on the center of the body, across the upper arms, upper legs, and right lower arm. Roll tiny balls of the remaining dough and position at intervals around the armor plates. If they don't easily stick in place, brush the dough with milk first.

5 Bake for 35–45 minutes until slightly risen and deeper in color. Using the tip of a sharp knife, cut a thin slit across the top of the head, then use a small teaspoon (or pastry bag) to pipe the HP or Hoisin sauce into the slit.

"THE MIRE ARE COMING

for each and every one of you. So what you going to do?"

TARDISH OF THE DAY

OOD HEAD BREAD

The Ood might look rather revolting with their squidlike tendrils, but they can be delicious in bread form if properly baked. This is a fun family bread to make—mildly spiced and tomatoey at one end and plain at the other. Don't worry too much about the shaping. If you get the eyes, ears, and tendrils in the right place, it'll look incredibly "Ood" like. If you've any dough leftover, shape it into balls and bake as mini bread rolls. Like most breads, this one freezes well too if you're planning a Doctor Who party and want to get ahead. Then all you need for your party are a few obliging Oods to hand out the drinks.

MAKES 1 LARGE LOAF

7 cups strong white bread flour,
   plus extra for dusting
1 tbsp active dry yeast
1 tbsp salt
4 tbsp olive oil
about 2½ cups warm water
2 tsp ground paprika
1 tbsp sundried tomato paste
1 tsp yeast extract paste
2 blueberries

YOU WILL NEED:
a 2-inch plain round cutter and a paintbrush

1 Put the flour, yeast, salt, oil, and almost all of the water in a large bowl and mix with a round-bladed knife to make a soft dough. Add the rest of the water if the dough feels dry and crumbly. Turn out onto a floured counter and knead for 10 minutes or until smooth and elastic. Return to a clean bowl and cover with plastic wrap. Leave in a warm place for about 1 hour or until doubled in size.

2 Turn the dough out onto the counter and cut off a third. Knead the paprika and tomato paste into the smaller portion on a floured counter. It'll become very sticky while you knead in the tomato paste, but will gradually become smooth and more manageable.

3 Grease a large baking sheet. Set aside 11 oz of the plain dough and shape the remainder into an egg shape for the Ood's head. Place on the baking sheet so the pointed end of the dough is in one corner of the baking sheet, giving you plenty of room to assemble the rest of the Ood diagonally across the baking sheet.

4 Pull off a small piece of the tomato-flavored dough and roll it into a long thin sausage under the palms of your hands until about 10 inches long. Push down onto the main section of the head on the baking sheet so it overlaps by 2½–3 inches. Curl the other end down toward the corner of the baking sheet. Make more tendrils in the same way, varying their length and thickness. You might not need all the tomato-flavored dough.

CONTINUES ON NEXT PAGE ▶

5 Take 3 oz of the reserved plain dough and cut in half. Roll under the palms of your hands into two thin sausages, each about 4 inches long. Position one on each side of the tendrils so the two tips meet at the nose end and the other ends are tucked under the bread. Secure in place with a dampened paintbrush.

6 Preheat the oven to 400°F. To finish the face, use large scissors to make deep snips into the dough about a third of the way up the sides of the face for ears. Take a ball of dough, about the size of a large tomato, and stretch into an oblong. Push down into the dough above the tendrils. Roll more dough under the palms of your hands to about a ½ inch thickness. Cut off a 1½-inch piece and press down into the dough across the base of the piece you've just added. Cut more strips, making each slightly wider than the previous, and position across the face until slightly higher than the level of the ears. Use the tip of a knife to score the area above the tendrils.

7 For the eyes, flatten more dough to a ¼ inch thickness on the counter and cut out a circle with a 2-inch plain round cutter. Cut into two semicircles. Press into the dough near the ears for the undersides of the eyes. Shape and position two thin strips of dough for the tops of the eyes.

8 Bake the bread for 25 minutes until risen and just firm. While baking, blend the yeast extract with a dash of water to thin the consistency. Brush over the face in and around the eyes, ears, and central area. Return to the oven for another 5–10 minutes until cooked through. Let cool on the baking sheet. Once cool, push a blueberry into the center of each eye.

"WE MUST FEED ... you— if you are hungry."

SLITHEEN CUISINE

The Slitheen from the planet Raxacoricofallapatorius are one of the scarier Doctor Who monsters of recent years. You probably won't be able to reproduce the "gas emissions" they make when pretending to be human, but choose an assortment of knobbly potatoes to bake and you'll be halfway there to making a rather impressive-looking Slitheen in its true, ugly form. Do make sure you leave the potatoes for about 15 minutes after baking so they're not too hot to handle, then you'll be able to squidge and mold them into shape. One Slitheen will serve three to four as part of a meal, but you could make two batches for a larger gathering.

MAKE 1 SLITHEEN

1 large baking potato, about
    14 oz
1 small baking potato, about
    7 oz
6 new potatoes in various sizes
1 tbsp olive or vegetable oil
3 large black olives, pitted
scant ½ cup whole cream cheese
1 tbsp green pesto
6 whole, small Guindilla peppers
    from a jar
a small piece of pita bread
1 slice Red Leicester
salt

YOU WILL NEED:
a paper pastry bag or plastic
food bag

1 Preheat the oven to 400°F. Pierce all the potatoes with a fork and rub with the oil. Sprinkle lightly with salt to season. Put the large potato in a small roasting pan and bake for 20 minutes, then add the medium potato and bake for 30 minutes. Add the new potatoes and bake for another 30–40 minutes until all the potatoes are tender. Leave until cool enough to handle.

2 Push the large potato down on a board using your thumbs to mold it into a body that sits upright. Transfer to a serving plate or board. Cut a thick slice off the thickest end of the small baking potato and set aside. Push in the sides of the potato with your fingers to shape the head. Use the tip of a knife to push a small mouth shape into the potato. You should be able to pinch the potato above the mouth to shape a small nose. Cut a slither of olive and push it into the mouth. Cut two large circles from the ends of the olives and secure in place with a dab of cream cheese to make the eyes.

CONTINUES ON NEXT PAGE ▶

3 Mix the remaining cream cheese with the pesto. Cut a cube shape from the piece of potato you've sliced off and position this on top of the body. Spoon the cream cheese into a paper pastry bag (or one corner of a plastic food bag). Twist the bag to secure the cream cheese in place and cut off a small tip. Pipe around the cube of potato to form a wrinkly neck. Position the head on top. If the head feels insecure, push a wooden toothpick down through the head and neck and into the body to hold it in shape.

4 Assemble the new potatoes on either side of the body to shape the long, gangly arms, starting with the lower arm sections on the board and building up the sections either side of the body. Squidge them together to hold them in place. For the potatoes that are either side of the shoulders, cut a small slice off so they sit snugly against the body. Secure in place if necessary with a dab of cream cheese. Cut long tips off the peppers to resemble claws and position at the ends of the arms.

5 For the neck gadget, cut a ¾ x ½-inch rectangle of pita bread. Cut a ½-inch square from the cheese (cut out the center if you can) and secure to the bread with a dab of cream cheese. Push gently into position at the neck.

"Have you got ANY VINEGAR?"

THE DOCTOR'S BLACKBOARD

The Twelfth Doctor likes his blackboard. He often jots down ideas or theories or strange symbols that probably make no sense at all to anyone else in the universe. To make this recipe look really effective, use a square or rectangular shallow baking dish with a rim to serve as the frame of the blackboard. Delicious on its own as a veggie supper, it also makes a tasty partner to chicken, lamb, sausages, or white fish.

SERVES 4–6

4 large eggplants
scant ½ cup olive oil
2 medium onions, chopped
1 fennel bulb, chopped
3 garlic cloves, crushed
two 14-oz cans of chopped
    tomatoes
1 tsp dried oregano
1 tsp superfine sugar
5-oz piece of rindless firm goat
    cheese
scant ¾ cup grated Parmesan
5 tbsp ready-made cheese sauce
salt and freshly ground black
    pepper

YOU WILL NEED:
a shallow square or rectangular
baking dish with a rim and a
plastic food bag

1 Preheat the oven to 375°F. Line two baking sheets with baking parchment.

2 Holding an eggplant vertically on the cutting board, cut a long, thick slice of skin from one side. Cut off about four more thick slices (set them aside) so you're left with the fleshy, skin-free center. Cut this into thick slices. Repeat with the remaining eggplants. Place all the "fleshy" eggplant slices in a single layer on the baking sheets and brush lightly with olive oil. Turn the slices over and brush with more oil. Season with a little salt and pepper and bake for 45 minutes, turning once halfway through cooking.

3 Heat the remaining oil in a large pan and gently fry the onions and fennel for 6–8 minutes until softened and beginning to color. Stir in the garlic, then the tomatoes, oregano, sugar, and a little seasoning. Cook gently for 25 minutes, stirring occasionally, until the sauce is thick and pulpy.

4 Cut a cylindrical shape from the firm center of the goat cheese to resemble a piece of chalk. Dice the remaining goat cheese.

CONTINUES ON NEXT PAGE ▶

"RUN, YOU CLEVER BOY and be a DOCTOR."

5 Set aside all the eggplant skin slices. Place half the baked "fleshy" eggplant slices in the base of a shallow square or rectangular baking dish with a rim. Spread half the tomato sauce on top and sprinkle with half the Parmesan cheese. Add the remaining baked "fleshy" eggplant slices, then the rest of the tomato sauce and Parmesan. Sprinkle the diced goat cheese on top. Finally, add the eggplant skin slices, if necessary cutting and patching together the slices so the filling is completely covered.

6 Cover the surface of the dish with foil, pressing it down firmly to flatten the filling. If you have a small metal baking dish that fits snugly inside the rim of the larger dish, position it on top and fill with ceramic baking beans or pie weights. This will help keep the surface of the "blackboard" flat. Bake for 30 minutes.

7 Heat the cheese sauce either in a small bowl in the microwave or in a small pan and stir until smooth. Let cool slightly and spoon into one corner of a plastic food bag. Twist the bag to contain the sauce and snip off the tip. Use the sauce to "scribble" words or symbols over the "blackboard." Add the goat cheese "chalk" and serve.

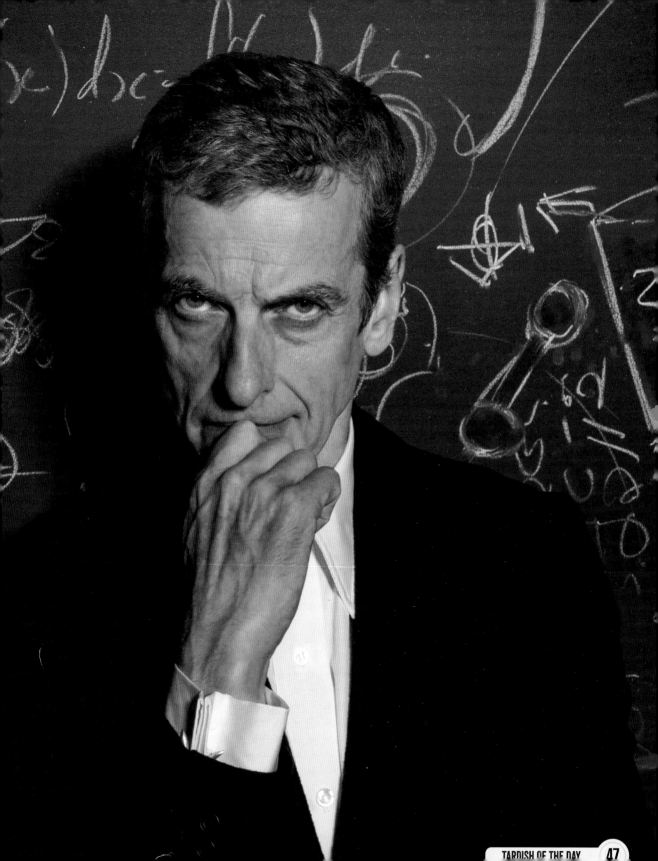

A PIZZA CASSANDRA

The Lady Cassandra O'Brien Dot Delta Seventeen may have had hundreds of cosmetic operations to achieve that perfect flat figure of hers, but you can achieve a similar result with some ready-made puff pastry—a great base for a cheesy pizza topping. It's so easy to shape the scalloped edge to resemble Cassandra, stretched in her silver frame and all the more effective if you serve it in a ridged aluminum or stainless-steel baking tray. Just don't let her dry out, or cracks may appear ...

SERVES 4

1-lb 2-oz pack of puff pastry
all-purpose flour, for dusting
1 red bell pepper, seeded
2 tbsp olive oil
1 onion, chopped
14-oz can of chopped tomatoes
½ tsp dried oregano
3 tbsp tomato ketchup
1½ cups ready-made cheese sauce
3½ oz Gruyère
1 cucumber slice, halved
1 black grape
salt and freshly ground black pepper

YOU WILL NEED:
a 4–4¼-inch plain round cutter

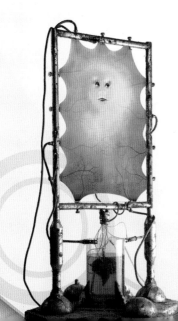

1 Preheat the oven to 400°F. Grease a large aluminum or stainless-steel baking sheet or tray, preferably ridged.

2 Roll out the pastry on a lightly floured counter to a rectangle measuring about 15 x 12 inches or as big as your baking sheet will contain. Using a 4–4¼-inch plain round cutter, cut out two scalloped edges from one short side of the rectangle and three from each long side. Use a knife to cut off one long curve from the remaining short end. This will be the base. Slice off the corners.

3 Transfer the pastry to the baking sheet. Use the tip of the knife to cut a shallow groove all around the edges of the pastry, about ½ inch in from the edges. Prick the base with a fork and bake for 20 minutes until puffed and golden. Flatten the risen center down with the back of a spoon.

4 For Cassandra's face, cut a mouth from the red bell pepper, making it about 2 inches wide and 1 inch tall at the widest point. Put to one side and dice the remaining red bell pepper.

5 Heat the oil in a pan and fry the onion and chopped bell pepper for 5 minutes to soften. Stir in the tomatoes, oregano, and a little seasoning. Bring to a boil, reduce the heat, and simmer gently for 10 minutes, stirring frequently, until thick and pulpy. Let cool.

6 Stir the ketchup into the tomato sauce and spread into the pastry shell in an even layer. If the cheese sauce is thick, give it a good stir to loosen it up. Spread in an even layer over the tomato base. Grate the cheese on top.

7 Bake the pizza for 25 minutes or until the cheese is melted and bubbling, but not turning brown. Position the red pepper mouth and two semicircles of cucumber for eyes. Cut two slices of grape, then cut a thin slice off each and position in the center of the cucumber pieces. Let stand for 15 minutes before serving to let the sauce cool and thicken a little. Serve with a leafy salad.

ZYGON PIE

As we know, the Zygons are already here. Anyone could be a Zygon as they can disguise themselves to blend into human society. Though they probably wouldn't disguise themselves as a tasty pie! This is a delicious sausage and vegetable pie wrapped in a puff pastry shell, though the decoration of the pie resembles the reddish, reptilian, suckered skin of the Zygon monster. All you need to accompany it is a leafy salad.

SERVES 6–8

1 lb 10 oz sweet potatoes, scrubbed, cut into small cubes
2 large red onions, coarsely chopped
2 tbsp olive oil
2 garlic cloves, chopped
1 lb 2 oz lean sausage meat
1 tsp dried oregano
3 tsp sundried tomato paste
two 1-lb 2-oz packs of puff pastry
all-purpose flour, for dusting
1 medium egg yolk
freshly ground black pepper

1 Preheat the oven to 375°F. Grease a large baking sheet. Scatter the sweet potato cubes in a roasting pan with the onion. Drizzle with the oil and roast for 45 minutes until the potatoes are tender, turning the ingredients once during cooking. Add the garlic and roast for another 5 minutes. Let cool.

2 Put the sausage meat into a bowl with the oregano, 2 tsp of the tomato paste and plenty of freshly ground black pepper. Mix well.

3 Roll out each block of pastry on a lightly floured counter to a 14 x 12-inch rectangle. Cut out a 12 x 10-inch oval shape from one piece and transfer to the baking sheet. Set aside the trimmings. Cut out a slightly larger oval shape from the other rectangle. This should measure about 13 x 11 inches. Brush the edges of the pastry oval on the baking sheet with water. Arrange the sweet potato mixture over the pastry, leaving a ¾-inch rim of pastry around the edges. Distribute the sausage meat mixture on top, doming it up slightly in the center. Position the second pastry oval on top, pressing it down firmly around the edges and trimming off any excess pastry.

CONTINUES ON NEXT PAGE

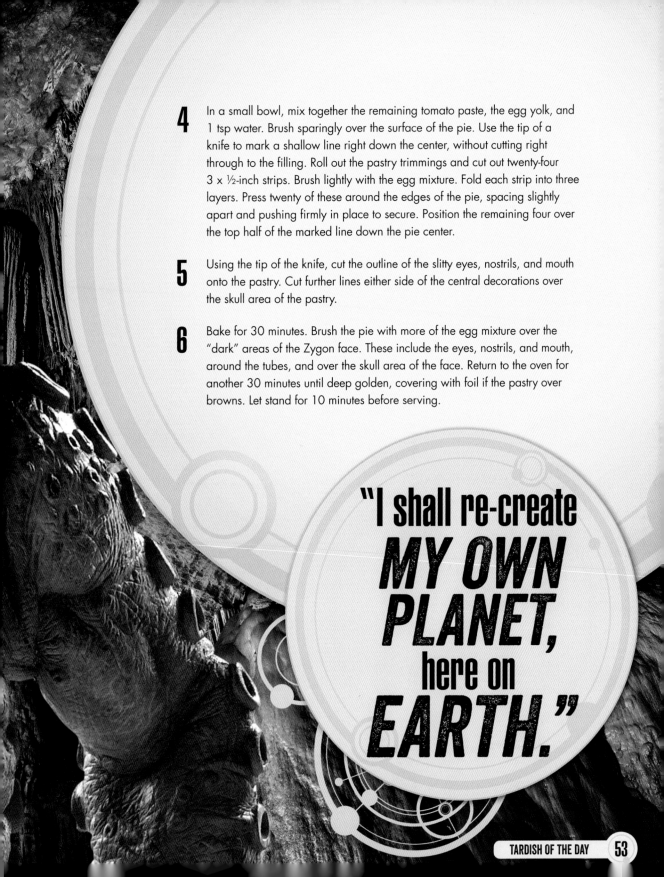

4 In a small bowl, mix together the remaining tomato paste, the egg yolk, and 1 tsp water. Brush sparingly over the surface of the pie. Use the tip of a knife to mark a shallow line right down the center, without cutting right through to the filling. Roll out the pastry trimmings and cut out twenty-four 3 x ½-inch strips. Brush lightly with the egg mixture. Fold each strip into three layers. Press twenty of these around the edges of the pie, spacing slightly apart and pushing firmly in place to secure. Position the remaining four over the top half of the marked line down the pie center.

5 Using the tip of the knife, cut the outline of the slitty eyes, nostrils, and mouth onto the pastry. Cut further lines either side of the central decorations over the skull area of the pastry.

6 Bake for 30 minutes. Brush the pie with more of the egg mixture over the "dark" areas of the Zygon face. These include the eyes, nostrils, and mouth, around the tubes, and over the skull area of the face. Return to the oven for another 30 minutes until deep golden, covering with foil if the pastry over browns. Let stand for 10 minutes before serving.

"I shall re-create MY OWN PLANET, here on EARTH."

WHO-GAZY HANDMINES

If you were trapped in a field of handmines, it would be great if you could just eat your way out. Of course, the young Davros didn't have that option and had to rely on the Doctor to save him. Or not. A lovely potato-topped family fish pie makes an effective base for that handmine scene and is like a stargazy fish pie, except this one has hand shapes instead of fish heads sticking out of it. Black seeds such as sesame, nigella, and mustard add a dark and mysterious "earthiness."

SERVES 4–5

1 lb 2 oz white fish,
   such as cod, haddock, pollack,
   skinned weight
3 tbsp milk
4 medium eggs, soft-boiled
   and shelled
12 large fresh or frozen peeled
   raw shrimp
2 lb mealy potatoes
3½ tbsp butter
1 tbsp mild olive or vegetable oil
1 fennel bulb, chopped
3 tbsp chopped dill
1¼ cups ready-made cheese sauce
½ packed cup grated Cheddar
2 tbsp nigella seeds, mustard seeds
   or black sesame seeds
salt and freshly ground
   black pepper

YOU WILL NEED:
a 3½-inch hand cookie cutter

1 Check over the fish for any bones. Put in a frying pan, add the milk and a little seasoning, and cover with a lid. Cook gently for 10 minutes or until the fish is just cooked. Transfer to a pie dish, flaking the fish into chunky pieces. Tuck the whole eggs between the fish chunks and scatter with the shrimp.

2 Cut five or six ½-inch- thick slices from the largest potatoes and stamp out hand shapes using a 3½-inch hand cookie cutter. Set aside. Cut the trimmings and the rest of the potatoes into chunks and cook in a pan of boiling, lightly salted water for 12 minutes until tender. Drain and return to the pan. Mash well and stir in 2 tbsp of the butter and a little seasoning.

3 Preheat the oven to 375°F. Melt the remaining butter with the oil in a frying pan and gently fry the potato hand shapes for 5 minutes, turning once, until pale golden. Lift out onto a plate and gently fry the fennel for 5 minutes to soften. Stir in the dill and scatter into the pie dish. Spoon the cheese sauce on top. Spoon the mash over the sauce and spread roughly with a fork. Sprinkle with the cheese.

4 Sprinkle the hand shapes with some of the seeds. Bake the pie for 15 minutes. Remove from the oven and push the potato hands into the top of the pie so they stand upright. Sprinkle with the remaining seeds and bake for another 30–40 minutes until the surface is bubbling and golden. Serve with peas.

"Survival is just **A CHOICE.** Choose it **NOW.**"

"INSIDE A DALEK" SALAD

The Doctor once described the Dalek creature inside the casing as "a living, bubbling lump of hate." For many years the actual Dalek creature wasn't shown in full on television—just a claw here or a glimpse of something nasty there. But now we know what the Dalek creature looks like, and here's how you can make your own, although it won't actually be living or bubbling. With a little imagination, a tasty salad or lunchbox can be made to resemble the grossest matter inside a Dalek. Vegetable ribbons, noodles, some tendrilly squid, and dyed eggs really do work well and taste so good. Try to forget the inspiration behind this dish when you eat it!

SERVES 2

2 tbsp red or white wine vinegar
2 tsp red food coloring
4 medium eggs
4 scallions
2 oz wholewheat noodles
2 zucchini
2 carrots
3½-oz ready-made squid or
    octopus salad (optional)
4 tbsp mayonnaise
1 small garlic clove, crushed
good pinch of chili powder
1 tsp soy sauce

1 Put the vinegar and food coloring in a small pan with 3 cups water and bring to a gentle simmer. Add the eggs and cook gently for 4 minutes. Lift the eggs out on a spoon and run under cold water so they're cool enough to handle. Using the back of a teaspoon, gently crack each egg all over so the shells are shattered, but not falling apart. Return to the pan and simmer for another 2 minutes. Turn off the heat and let the eggs cool in the liquid, then remove the shells.

2 Trim and cut the scallions lengthwise into thin strips. Bring a small pan of water to a boil, add the scallion strips, and cook for 30 seconds. Lift out with a slotted spoon into a bowl and add the noodles to the pan. Cook gently until tender. Drain thoroughly and add to the bowl.

3 Shape the zucchini and carrots into ribbons. An inexpensive spiral cutter is ideal for this. If you don't have one, coarsely grate the vegetables or use the shredder attachment of a food processor. Add to the bowl with the squid or octopus salad, if using. Bury the shelled eggs into the salad.

4 Combine the mayonnaise, garlic, chili powder, and soy sauce in a small bowl. Dot over the salad and combine very lightly so the salad looks a bit gooey in places.

PICNIC AT ASGARD

No records survive of exactly what the Doctor and River Song had to eat when they went on their picnic at Asgard. It is also not entirely clear if this was the Asgard of Norse mythology, one of the Nine Worlds and home to the Aesir gods, or whether it was the Asgard crater on Jupiter's moon Callisto. The crater seems more likely, but with the Doctor and River you never quite know. But whatever they ate, and wherever they were, you can be sure they would have loved this delicious pie.

SERVES 8

1-lb 2-oz pack of puff pastry
all-purpose flour, for dusting
1 tsp vegetable oil
1 onion, chopped
1¾ lb skinless, boneless chicken
    breasts, cut into large chunks
1 tsp dried oregano
1 tsp fennel seeds, crushed
1 tsp salt
1 lb 2 oz cooked ham, in one
    piece, about ¾ inch thick
beaten egg, to glaze
freshly ground black pepper

YOU WILL NEED:
a loaf pan with bottom
measurements of 7 x 3½ inches,
pie weights, ceramic baking beans,
or dried beans reserved for baking
blind, a 2-inch heart-shaped cutter,
and a meat thermometer, if you
have one

1 Preheat the oven to 400°F. Thinly roll out 12 oz of the pastry on a lightly floured counter and use to line the bottom and sides of a loaf pan with bottom measurements of 7 x 3½ inches. The pastry should come up the sides of the pan and overhang the edges by at least 1¼ inches to allow for it to shrink back. Press the pastry firmly up the sides and into the corners, squeezing the creases in the pastry firmly into the ends of the pan.

2 Line the pastry with foil, pushing it firmly into the corners, up the sides, and over the top edges of the pan. The foil will hold the pastry in place as it bakes. Fill the bottom with pie weights or baking beans (you can also use dried beans reserved for baking blind). Bake for 30 minutes. Remove the foil and beans and press the pastry back against the sides of the pan. Reduce the oven temperature to 325°F.

3 For the filling, heat the oil in a small frying pan and fry the onion for 5 minutes to soften. Transfer to a bowl. Finely chop the chicken in a food processor. Add to the bowl with the oregano, fennel, and salt. Season with black pepper and mix well.

4 Using a 2-inch heart-shaped cutter, cut shapes out of the ham. Cut the shapes close together so you have enough hearts and don't waste too much ham. If the cutter is hard to press through the ham, tap it gently with a rolling pin.

CONTINUES ON NEXT PAGE

"Life with a **TIME TRAVELER.** Never knew it could be such *HARD WORK.*"

5 Press half the chicken mixture into the pastry-lined pan and push a deep groove along the center of the chicken. Press the heart shapes down into the groove in the chicken filling, packing them closely one behind the other right down the length of the pan. Spoon the remaining chicken mixture around the sides and over the top of the ham.

6 Trim off the excess pastry around the top of the pan, leaving enough of a pastry rim to support the lattice decoration. Brush the pastry edges with beaten egg. Thinly roll out the remaining pastry and cut into ⅝-inch- wide strips. Use to make a lattice decoration over the top of the pie. Brush the top with more beaten egg.

7 Bake for 1½ hours or until the pastry is golden and the chicken feels firm when you push a skewer down into it. Use a meat thermometer if you have one. It should register at least 180°F. Leave the pie in the pan to firm up and serve warm or cold in thick slices.

THE IMPOSSIBLE GIRL'S IMPOSSIBLE RECIPE

Clara, "the impossible girl," strived to cook a baked soufflé. Although she didn't know it, she had been turned into a Dalek at the time, which probably explains her rather limited success and why we saw her tipping a failed attempt into the garbage! Hot soufflés have a reputation for being difficult because a light touch is needed to keep the mixture aerated and, of course, they sink so quickly after baking. Fingers crossed that this delicious raspberry soufflé will not only be possible, but perfect!

SERVES 6

butter, for greasing
½ cup superfine sugar, plus extra
    for coating
2 tsp cornstarch
2 cups fresh or frozen raspberries
squeeze of lemon juice
4 medium egg whites
confectioners' sugar, for dusting
pouring cream, to serve

YOU WILL NEED:
six 5-oz individual soufflé dishes

1 Thoroughly grease six 5-oz individual soufflé dishes with the butter. Sprinkle a little superfine sugar over the butter, tilting the dishes so they're evenly coated in sugar. Chill.

2 Mix the cornstarch in a pan with 2 tbsp water. Add the raspberries and lemon juice and slowly bring to a simmer, crushing the raspberries with the edge of the spoon and stirring until the mixture has thickened slightly. Press through a strainer into a bowl, scraping the mixture from the underside of the strainer so you don't waste any.

3 Preheat the oven to 350°F. Whisk the egg whites in a thoroughly clean bowl until softly peaking. Gradually whisk in the remaining superfine sugar, a spoonful at a time, until thick and glossy. Spoon a quarter of the meringue over the raspberries and fold in gently with a large metal spoon to lighten it. Fold in the remainder.

4 Divide the mixture among the dishes and level the tops. Place on a baking sheet and bake for 20 minutes. Dust lightly with confectioners' sugar and serve immediately with cream.

EGGS-STIR-MIX-BAKE

(SAY IT FAST AND LIKE A DALEK ...)

EXTERMI-CAKE

The Daleks may be the most evil and ruthless life form in the universe, but with a bit of care and effort, a Dalek can also be made into a delicious and impressive cake. Ideally, make the sponge cake a day in advance so it can firm up a little before cutting and shaping.

SERVES 12–15

5 small, very ripe bananas
1 1/3 cups unsalted butter, softened
1½ packed cups light brown sugar
4 medium eggs, beaten
2 tsp vanilla extract
3 cups self-rising flour

TO FINISH:

¾ cup + 1 tsp or 1½ sticks unsalted butter, softened
2 cups confectioners' sugar, plus extra for dusting
1 tsp vanilla extract
5 oz gray ready-to-roll icing
2¼ lb white ready-to-roll icing, colored a pale, warm brown with a mix of brown and yellow paste food colorings
edible gold food spray
5 oz black ready-to-roll icing
silver food coloring
3 candy sticks
small bit of yellow ready-to-roll icing

YOU WILL NEED:

a 33-oz and a14-oz ovenproof bowl, a 9-inch round cake board, a 4-inch plain round cutter, and a fine paintbrush

1 Preheat the oven to 325°F. Grease a 33-oz and a 14-oz ovenproof bowl and line the bottoms with circles of baking parchment. Cut a long strip of baking parchment measuring 22 x 6 inches and fold in half lengthwise. Fit around the top of the large bowl so the paper extends the rim by 1½ inches. Secure the overlap in place with tape or a paper clip and grease the inside of the paper collar. (The collar will prevent the cake batter spilling over the top of the bowl as it bakes).

2 Mash the peeled bananas in a small bowl. Beat together the butter and brown sugar in a large bowl until pale and creamy. Gradually beat in the eggs, a little at a time. Stir in the bananas and vanilla. Add half the flour and fold in gently with a large metal spoon. Fold in the remainder. Spoon 2¼ lb of the batter into the large bowl and the rest into the smaller bowl. Bake the small bowl for 45 minutes and the large one for 1¼ hours. The cakes are cooked when they feel firm and a skewer inserted in the center comes out clean. Let cool in the bowls for 15 minutes.

3 Loosen the edges of the cakes with a knife and turn out onto a wire rack to cool completely. Beat together the butter, confectioners' sugar, and vanilla extract until pale and creamy. Position the cakes with their flat tops face down on the surface. Using a sharp knife, trim the sides off the small cake so they're straight rather than curved. Trim the sides off the larger cake in the same way. The diameter of the cake base should be about 5 inches. Cut the small cake vertically in half and the larger cake into three. Sandwich all the layers back together using most of the buttercream. Re-assemble the layers so the cake is almost vertical on one side (this will form the back of the Dalek) and sloping at the front. Secure the small cake on top of the large with a little more buttercream. Spread the remaining buttercream all over the cake.

CONTINUES ON NEXT PAGE ▶

4 Dampen a 9-inch round cake board with water. Thinly roll out the gray icing on a counter dusted with confectioners' sugar and lay the icing over the board. Smooth out with the palms of your hands and trim off the excess around the edges.

5 For the domed top of the Dalek, take 5 oz of the brown-colored icing and knead into a smooth ball. Flatten out on a lightly dusted counter until 4 inches in diameter. To get a really neat edge, flatten the icing out to a slightly larger round and cut through with a 4-inch round cutter. Position on top of the cake and ease slightly down the sides. Spray with a little edible gold spray.

6 For the grill, take 3 oz of the black icing and roll out until large enough to cut out four 11 x ½-inch strips. Wrap one strip around the cake so the lower edge of the strip is 1½ inches lower than the bottom edge of the brown icing, pressing gently into the buttercream to secure. Cut off any excess icing at the back. Position the three remaining strips in the same way, overlapping the strips slightly so the final strip meets the brown icing.

7 Set aside 3½ oz of the brown icing. For the skirt, roll out the remainder to a 20 x 6-inch rectangle. Neaten one long side with a knife and wrap the icing around the cake so the neatened edge meets the grill. Smooth the icing down, overlapping it slightly at the back and securing the overlap in place with a damp paintbrush. Trim off the excess around the base. Use the trimmings to patch up any gaps in the icing at the back of the cake. Lightly spray the skirt area with more gold spray. As you do this, hold a piece of card or paper against the grill so you don't get any on the black icing. Carefully transfer the cake to the cake board (this is easiest done by lowering it gently in place with a spatula). Roll out the remaining black icing until large enough to cut out a 18 x ¾-inch strip. Secure around the base of the Dalek for the bumper. Set aside the trimmings.

8 Roll out half the reserved brown icing until large enough to cut out two 12 x ½-inch strips. Secure around the "waist" of the cake, leaving a small gap in between the strips.

9 Mark vertical panels around the icing skirt using the back of a knife. Shape small balls of the reserved brown icing, about the size of a pea, and flatten. Position four pieces in each of the panels. Use silver food coloring and a fine paintbrush to paint the brown strips around the middle of the cake and all the small round decorations.

10 For the eye stalk, push one candy stick into the dome so 1 inch is visible. Decorate with black icing, pushing a ball of icing onto the end and adding an even smaller ball of yellow icing to the end. Push a small "plunger"-shaped piece of black icing onto the end of another candy stick and push into the cake until sufficiently supported. Wrap a flat piece of white icing around the remaining candy stick to shape the gun stick. Push slightly further into the cake. Paint the gun with silver food coloring. Shape two small lights in white icing and secure to the top of the dome.

DALEKTABLE ARMY

Daleks don't eat—or at least, not in the way that we do. But if they did, they'd certainly enjoy these delicious cupcakes. Silver cupcake liners, candy sticks, and candies make an easy and effective decoration for these Dalek teatime cakes. Both the sponge and topping are flavored with coconut, but you can easily substitute another flavoring like vanilla, orange, or lemon instead.

MAKES 10 CAKES

$^2/_3$ cup slightly salted butter, softened
scant 1 cup superfine sugar
3 medium eggs
$1^1/_3$ cups self-rising flour
2 oz creamed coconut

TO DECORATE:
¾ cup + 2 tbsp or 1¾ sticks slightly salted butter, softened
scant $2^1/_3$ cups confectioners' sugar
1½ tsp coconut extract
black food coloring
blue mini candy-covered chocolates
10 small black gummy candies
10 candy sticks
small bit of white ready-to-roll icing
tube of black writing icing

YOU WILL NEED:
a 12-cup cupcake tray and a 12-cup mini cupcake tray with foil cupcake liners

1 Preheat the oven to 350°F. Line 10 sections of a 12-cup cupcake tray with foil cupcake liners. Fit 10 foil mini cupcake liners into a mini cupcake tray (if you don't have a mini cupcake tray, use double layer liners and arrange on a baking sheet; the extra layer will stop the liners collapsing as they bake). Put the butter, superfine sugar, eggs, and flour in a bowl. If the coconut is very solid, grate it into the bowl. If slightly softened, it's easier to finely chop it and add. Beat the ingredients together for a couple of minutes until pale and creamy.

2 Divide among the paper liners, filling them no more than two-thirds full. Bake the larger cupcakes for 17–20 minutes and the smaller ones for 12 minutes. The cakes should be risen and just firm to the touch. Transfer to a wire rack to cool completely.

3 For the buttercream, beat together the butter, confectioners' sugar, and coconut extract until pale and creamy. Beat in a little black food coloring until it is pale gray.

4 Pile the buttercream on top of the large cupcakes. Smooth out with a palette knife to a deep, dome shape. Invert a small cupcake on top and smooth the buttercream out to fill any gaps between the cakes.

5 Press vertical rows of the blue candies around the cakes. Push a small black candy onto one end of each candy stick and press into the cakes, just under the small cupcake liners. Roll pea-size balls of white icing and flatten slightly. Secure to the small cupcake liners with a dot of black writing icing for the eye stalks. Pipe further dots of black icing over the white.

COOK'S TIPS

If the black candies are very hard you can soften them in the microwave. Do this very briefly and one at a time in short spurts. Take care as they will quickly overheat. If you can't get hold of small candies, shape black ready-to-roll icing instead.

"SEEK LOCATE TERMINATE"

SWEET SILENCE

Luckily this cake isn't like the real Silence. So if you get distracted while making it and look away, you won't immediately forget what you were doing. The success of the cake relies largely on getting a good sponge shape before you cover it with icing. Bake the cake in an ovenproof mixing bowl so you start with a domed cake, ready for cutting into shape. Allow plenty of time for the decoration. This is a creation you'll get thoroughly absorbed in—and love the results!

SERVES 12

1 1/3 cups slightly salted butter, softened
1 2/3 cups superfine sugar
1 tbsp vanilla extract
5 medium eggs, beaten
2¾ cups + 1½ tbsp self-rising flour

TO FINISH:

2/3 cup slightly salted butter
1½ cups confectioners' sugar, plus extra for dusting
6–8 tbsp strawberry or raspberry jam
2 lb flesh-colored ready-to-roll icing (see Cook's tips on page 78)
burgundy food coloring powder
small bit of red ready-to-roll icing
black food coloring

YOU WILL NEED:

a large 3-quart mixing bowl, a fine paintbrush, and a pastry brush

1 Preheat the oven to 325°F. Grease a large mixing bowl with a capacity of 3 quarts. Line the bottom with a large circle of baking parchment. Beat the butter, superfine sugar, and vanilla extract in a bowl until pale and creamy. Gradually beat in the eggs, a little at a time. If the mixture starts to separate, beat in a spoonful of the flour.

2 Sift the flour into the bowl and fold in gently until combined. Turn into the prepared bowl and level the surface. Bake for about 1¼–1½ hours or until the surface is just firm to the touch. A skewer inserted into the center should come out clean. Let cool completely in the bowl.

3 Loosen the edges of the cake and invert out of the bowl. If the cake surface has risen in the center during baking, you'll need to slice this off so the cake sits flat on the surface with the rounded side face up.

4 To shape the face, you're aiming to create a sort of pear shape. First cut two slices off the sides of the cake, keeping the knife vertical but angling the cuts so the cake is narrower at the "chin." The Silence has a bony area around the center of the face, so keep the hard edge of the cut for the central third of the face and round off the edge over the top third for the skull and the bottom third for the chin. (All the pieces of cake you've cut away will freeze well for a trifle another time).

CONTINUES ON NEXT PAGE ▶

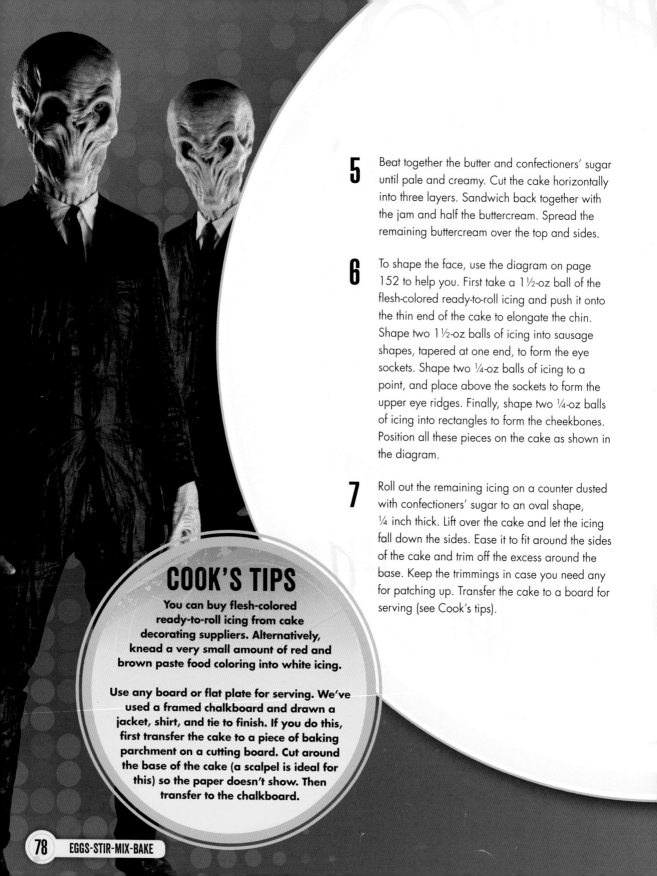

5 Beat together the butter and confectioners' sugar until pale and creamy. Cut the cake horizontally into three layers. Sandwich back together with the jam and half the buttercream. Spread the remaining buttercream over the top and sides.

6 To shape the face, use the diagram on page 152 to help you. First take a 1½-oz ball of the flesh-colored ready-to-roll icing and push it onto the thin end of the cake to elongate the chin. Shape two 1½-oz balls of icing into sausage shapes, tapered at one end, to form the eye sockets. Shape two ¼-oz balls of icing to a point, and place above the sockets to form the upper eye ridges. Finally, shape two ¼-oz balls of icing into rectangles to form the cheekbones. Position all these pieces on the cake as shown in the diagram.

7 Roll out the remaining icing on a counter dusted with confectioners' sugar to an oval shape, ¼ inch thick. Lift over the cake and let the icing fall down the sides. Ease it to fit around the sides of the cake and trim off the excess around the base. Keep the trimmings in case you need any for patching up. Transfer the cake to a board for serving (see Cook's tips).

COOK'S TIPS

You can buy flesh-colored ready-to-roll icing from cake decorating suppliers. Alternatively, knead a very small amount of red and brown paste food coloring into white icing.

Use any board or flat plate for serving. We've used a framed chalkboard and drawn a jacket, shirt, and tie to finish. If you do this, first transfer the cake to a piece of baking parchment on a cutting board. Cut around the base of the cake (a scalpel is ideal for this) so the paper doesn't show. Then transfer to the chalkboard.

8 While the icing is still soft and pliable, mold it around the eyes and lower face. Ease the icing carefully into the eye sockets so you don't tear it (though if you do, you can patch it up). Use the handle tip of a paintbrush to press the nose shape into the icing and to add further lines, cracks, and crannies.

9 Use a dry pastrybrush to brush the burgundy food coloring powder into the eye areas and lightly over other areas of the cake to accentuate the bony shape. (Practice on a little leftover icing first.) Use a fine paintbrush to paint the grooves and nose.

10 Take two pea-size balls of red icing and flatten into oval shapes for the eyes. Position right at the top of the eye sockets. Paint the centers black, leaving a fine red rim.

SALLY SPARROW'S WEEPING ANGEL CAKE

The first encounter that Sally Sparrow had with a Weeping Angel was in a spooky old house where she found a warning message from the Doctor hidden under the wallpaper. Sadly, it wasn't edible wallpaper, but the message was still effective. The idea behind this creation has to be an angel cake even if the Weeping Angel is far from angelic! The cake is layered up with cream cheese frosting and decorated with ready-to-roll icing—another opportunity to show off your creative skills. The cake base can be made a few days in advance and freezes well. Once layered up with cream cheese frosting and decorated, it should be stored in a cool place and served within 2 days.

SERVES 12

8 medium egg whites
1 tsp cream of tartar
finely grated zest of 2 lemons
¼ tsp salt
1 cup superfine sugar
²/₃ cup all-purpose flour

FOR THE FROSTING:
1¾ cups whole cream cheese
1 cup confectioners' sugar
1 tsp lemon juice
3½ tbsp butter, very soft

TO DECORATE:
1 lb 2 oz white ready-to-roll icing
green, brown, and black paste food
  colorings
5 tbsp confectioners' sugar, plus
  extra for dusting

YOU WILL NEED:
a 13 x 8½-inch jelly roll pan
or similar-size shallow pan,
a paintbrush, and a paper
pastry bag or plastic food
bag

1 Preheat the oven to 325°F. Grease a 13 x 8½-inch jelly roll pan or similar-size shallow pan and line with baking parchment. Put the egg whites in a large, thoroughly clean bowl and whisk until frothy. Add the cream of tartar, lemon zest, and salt and whisk until the egg whites are softly peaking. Sprinkle in 2 heaping teaspoonfuls of the superfine sugar and whisk briefly to mix. Continue to add the superfine sugar, a heaping spoonful at a time, whisking well after each addition.

2 Sift the flour onto a piece of paper towel. Sift again, this time into the bowl. Fold in with a large metal spoon until combined. Spoon half the batter into the pan and spread level. Bake for 15 minutes until just firm to the touch. Carefully slide the cake and paper out of the pan. Reline the pan and bake the remaining batter in the same way. Let cool.

CONTINUES ON NEXT PAGE ▶

3 For the frosting, beat the cream cheese in a bowl until softened. Add the confectioners' sugar, lemon juice, and butter and beat until completely smooth. Cut each of the cakes in half widthwise and place one layer on a serving board. Set aside a third of the frosting and use the remainder to sandwich the cake layers together on the board. Position the top layer of cake so the flat base is uppermost. Spread the remaining frosting over the top and sides.

4 Take 7 oz of the ready-to-roll icing and knead on the counter to soften slightly. Knead in a dash of green food coloring, a dash of brown, and a dash of black until the icing is streaked with color. Thinly roll out on a counter dusted with confectioners' sugar and cut out a rectangle that's large enough to cover the top and long sides of the cake. Lift over the cake, smooth out gently, and trim off any excess.

5 For the peeling wallpaper, take a ½-oz piece of white icing and roll out as thinly as you can. Tear off small pieces and secure to the top and bottom of the cake with a dampened paintbrush to resemble raggedy patches of peeled paper. Add a couple of pieces to the board too.

6 For the wallpaper, knead more green and black coloring into the remaining white icing until a deep, dark green. Thinly roll out half the icing and lay diagonally over the left hand side of the cake as in the photograph. Fit the icing down the sides and trim off the excess around the base. Roll out the remaining icing and secure diagonally on the other side of the cake, fitting the icing down the sides. Use the icing trimmings to add further sections of wallpaper, keeping the edges raggedy as though peeled away from the base. Crumple up more trimmings and scatter onto the board.

7 Put the confectioners' sugar in a bowl and stir in a few drops of water to make a thin paste. Transfer to a paper pastry bag or one corner of a plastic food bag and snip off the merest tip. Use to pipe the wallpaper design.

8 Dilute a little black paste food coloring with water so it has the consistency of thick paint. Using a fine paintbrush, paint the words onto the icing as shown in the photograph.

"DON'T BLINK
Don't even blink.
Blink and you're
DEAD."

TIME AND RELATIVE DIMENSIONS IN CAKE

Wherever and whenever he ends up, the Doctor almost certainly got there in the TARDIS. It can travel anywhere in time and space. But wherever he ends up, you can be sure he'll soon be in trouble … This birthday cake depicts the TARDIS tumbling through space on Doctor Who's latest time traveling mission. A moist and fruity carrot cake on the inside, it's a vision of sparkling space dust on the outside. Carrot cake keeps well once frosted, so you can make it several days ahead of the party.

SERVES 12–15

9 oz carrots

1 cup + 2 tbsp or 2¼ sticks slightly salted butter, softened

1¼ cups light brown sugar

2 tsp vanilla extract

4 medium eggs, beaten

scant 2½ cups self-rising flour

2 tsp baking powder

2 tsp ground mixed spice

1¼ cups ground almonds

¾ cup golden raisins

TO DECORATE:

$^2/_3$ cup slightly salted butter, softened

1½ cups confectioners' sugar, plus extra for dusting

14 oz dark blue ready-to-roll icing

1 oz orange ready-to-roll icing

9 oz white ready-to-roll icing

1 mini marshmallow

9 oz black ready-to-roll icing

edible gold and silver glitter

YOU WILL NEED:

a large 3-quart mixing bowl, an empty 14-oz or 7-oz food can (such as for condensed milk or canned tomatoes), a paintbrush, and a paper pastry bag fitted with a writing tip

CONTINUES ON NEXT PAGE

"It's a telephone box from the 1950s. **IT'S A DISGUISE.**"

1. Preheat the oven to 325°F. Grease a large mixing bowl with a capacity of 3 quarts. Remove both ends from an empty food can. Wash, then grease and line the bottom and sides with baking parchment. Place the can on a small baking sheet lined with baking parchment. Line the bottom of the bowl with a large circle of baking parchment.

2. Finely grate the carrots. Beat the butter, brown sugar, and vanilla extract in a bowl until pale and creamy. Gradually beat in the eggs, a little at a time. If the mixture starts to separate, beat in a spoonful of the flour.

3. Add the flour, baking powder, mixed spice, and ground almonds and stir gently to combine. Stir in the golden raisins, and carrots. Spoon 5 oz of the cake batter into the food can. Spoon the remainder into the large bowl and level both surfaces. Bake the cake in the can for 30 minutes and the cake in the bowl for 1¼–1½ hours or until firm to the touch and a skewer inserted into the center comes out clean. Let cool completely in the can and bowl.

4. Loosen the edges of the large cake and invert onto a large round plate or board. Remove the cake from the can and peel away the paper. Cut off four sides so you end up with a tall square block for the TARDIS. Beat together the butter and confectioners' sugar until smooth and creamy. Spread a thin layer over the sides and top of the TARDIS and a thicker layer over the domed cake, making sure you fill the gap around the bottom of the cake.

5. Thinly roll out 5 oz of the dark blue icing on a counter lightly dusted with confectioners' sugar. Cut out four rectangles, one for each side of the TARDIS. Secure in place, pressing gently into the buttercream. Reroll the trimmings and cut out a square, slightly larger than the bottom of the TARDIS. Place on a square of baking parchment and spread a little buttercream in the center. Position the TARDIS on top. Cut another square of icing, the same size as the bottom, and secure to the top of the TARDIS. Reroll the trimmings and cut out a slightly smaller square. Position this on top of the roof, securing with a dampened paint brush.

6. Roll out a little orange icing as thinly as you can for the TARDIS windows. Cut small squares and secure in place. Add a smaller square of the white icing for the noticeboard. Secure a mini marshmallow to the roof, again with a dampened paintbrush. Put the reserved buttercream in a paper pastry bag fitted with a writing tip and use to pipe decorative lines over the TARDIS.

7. Roll out the black icing and the remaining white and blue icings under the palms of your hands, each into a long thick sausage. Squeeze the three colors together and roll again into a longer sausage shape. Fold and scrunch the icing together and reroll. Keep doing this for several more rolls until the colors start to marble and merge together. Roll out the icing with a rolling pin to a round large enough to cover the domed cake. Lift into position and smooth around the sides, trimming off the excess around the bottom.

8. Sprinkle the gold and silver glitter in trailing lines over the cake. If it doesn't stick, very lightly dampen the area you want to sprinkle over with a paintbrush first. Lightly brush the base of the TARDIS with water and secure to the top of the cake, slightly to one side of center. If you feel the TARDIS is a bit unbalanced, use a piece of bamboo skewer or cake pop stick to hold it in place.

CHRISTMAS SNOWMAN

Snowmen are usually happy, jolly-looking figures. But not the ones created by the Great Intelligence. They were really quite vicious, and didn't enter into the Christmas spirit at all. For Doctor Who fans looking for an alternative Christmas cake, this could be the answer— the snowman with the scary smile! It's a traditional rich fruit cake, finished with marzipan (almond paste) and royal icing so you can make it well in advance—job done!

SERVES 16–20

¾ cup + 2 tbsp or 1¾ sticks
    slightly salted butter, softened
1 cup dark brown sugar
2 tsp ground mixed spice
2 tsp ground ginger
finely grated zest and squeezed
    juice of 1 orange
3 medium eggs, beaten
1¾ cups + 2 tbsp all-purpose flour
1 lb 14 oz mixed dried fruit
¾ cup natural candied cherries,
    chopped
heaping ⅓ cup blanched
    almonds, chopped

TO DECORATE:

3 tbsp apricot jam
black paste food coloring
2¼ lb white marzipan
3–3½ cups confectioners' sugar,
    plus extra for dusting
2 medium egg whites
dried shredded coconut, to sprinkle

YOU WILL NEED:

a 2-quart and a 40-oz ovenproof
mixing bowl

1 Preheat the oven to 275°F. Grease a 2-quart and a 40-oz ovenproof mixing bowl and line the bottoms with circles of baking parchment. Put the butter, brown sugar, spices, and orange zest in a large bowl and beat with a handheld electric whisk until smooth and creamy. Gradually beat in the eggs, a little at a time, adding a spoonful of the flour if the mixture starts to separate. Stir in the orange juice. Fold in the flour, then the dried fruit, candied cherries, and almonds.

2 Spoon 2½ lb of the batter into the smaller bowl and level the surface. Spoon the remainder into the larger bowl. Bake the larger (but shallower) bowl for 1½ hours (as the bowl is shallower, the cake will cook faster) and the smaller bowl for 3 hours. The cakes are cooked when the surface feels firm and a skewer inserted into the center comes out clean. Let cool completely in the bowl.

3 Loosen the edges of the cakes with a knife and ease them out of the bowls. Invert the larger, shallow cake onto a serving plate or board. Using a sharp knife, round off the edges of the cake baked in the smaller bowl so it's reasonably round. Position on top of the other cake.

4 Melt the jam in a small pan with 1 tbsp water until softened. Press through a strainer and brush all over the surface of the cake.

CONTINUES ON NEXT PAGE ▶

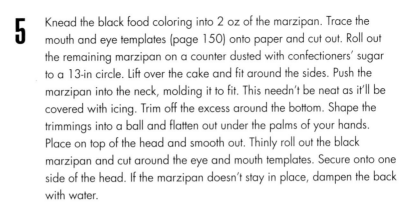

5 Knead the black food coloring into 2 oz of the marzipan. Trace the mouth and eye templates (page 150) onto paper and cut out. Roll out the remaining marzipan on a counter dusted with confectioners' sugar to a 13-in circle. Lift over the cake and fit around the sides. Push the marzipan into the neck, molding it to fit. This needn't be neat as it'll be covered with icing. Trim off the excess around the bottom. Shape the trimmings into a ball and flatten out under the palms of your hands. Place on top of the head and smooth out. Thinly roll out the black marzipan and cut around the eye and mouth templates. Secure onto one side of the head. If the marzipan doesn't stay in place, dampen the back with water.

6 Beat the egg whites in a bowl with 3 cups of the confectioners' sugar until completely smooth. The icing should form soft peaks. If the consistency is soft and losing its shape, beat in a little more confectioners' sugar. Spread a thick layer over the marzipan just above the mouth. Using the tip of a palette knife, pull the icing down at intervals over the mouth to resemble teeth. Spread the remaining icing around the rest of the mouth and the eyes, then over the rest of the cake. Smooth the icing down with a palette knife. Sprinkle coconut over the cake and board, and pat down lightly.

"Do you feel it? WINTER IS COMING."

PEEK-A-BOO PANDORICA

If the Doctor was surprised at what was inside the Pandorica when it opened, then your guests will be too. Though it won't be the Doctor himself—or even Amy Pond—inside, this impressively-sized cube-shaped cake would make a brilliant birthday cake for a Doctor Who fan of any age. Like the Pandorica itself, the cake is full of surprises when cut into as a feast of sweet treats spill out. The real Pandorica lasted for over 2,000 years, but ideally make the two cake bases and the sides for the box just 3 days before serving. You can then assemble and decorate the cake the day before.

SERVES 16–20

FOR THE CAKE:

1½ cups unsweetened cocoa
1 cup + 1 tbsp boiling water
12 oz semisweet chocolate, chopped
1⅓ cups slightly salted butter, softened
3 cups light brown sugar
6 medium eggs
scant 4¼ cups all-purpose flour
2 tsp baking soda

FOR THE BUTTERCREAM:

¾ cup + 1 tsp or 1½ sticks unsalted butter, softened
2 cups confectioners' sugar
¼ cup unsweetened cocoa

TO DECORATE:

4 lb dark gray ready-to-roll icing (see Cook's tips on page 94)
confectioners' sugar, for dusting
about 9 oz chocolates and sugar-coated candies, preferably green and blue
black food spray (optional)

YOU WILL NEED:

a 6-in square cake pan, an 4½-inch cutter, 10-inch, 9-inch, and 8-inch square silver cake boards, and a ⅝-inch wide gray ribbon

1 Preheat the oven to 325°F. Line a 6-inch square cake pan with a double thickness of wax paper. Grease the paper.

2 Put ¾ cup of the cocoa in a heatproof bowl. Pour the boiling water over the cocoa, whisking well until combined. Immediately tip in 6 oz of the chopped chocolate and leave until the chocolate has melted, stirring occasionally.

3 Put ⅔ cup of the butter, 3 cups of the brown sugar, 3 eggs, 2 cups of the flour, and 1 tsp baking soda in a large bowl and beat with a handheld electric whisk until smooth and creamy. Stir in the chocolate mixture until combined. Turn into the pan and level the surface. Bake for 1½–1¾ hours or until the cake feels firm to the touch and a skewer inserted into the center comes out clean. Let cool in the pan, then turn out onto a wire rack. Bake another chocolate cake using the remaining cake ingredients.

4 For the side panel decoration, line a baking sheet or board with baking parchment. Take a small piece of gray icing to practice the indentations as follows. It's best to lightly knead ready-to-roll icing first to make it more pliable. Collect three or four objects that have a small square or rectangular-shaped end. Metal cutlery, wooden chopsticks, giant matchsticks, and even the end of a small pencil sharpener are ideal. Try pressing a line of these into the icing you've rolled to see if the shapes are convincing for the Pandorica.

5 Roll out 7 oz of the gray icing on a counter dusted with confectioners' sugar. Keep the icing as square as possible in shape and roll out until you're able to cut out a neat 6-inch square (see Cook's tips on page 94). It's easier if you transfer the icing to the baking parchment before cutting so it holds its shape. Gently impress an 4½-inch plain round cutter into the icing to mark, but not cut through, a circle. Gently press the items you've collected into the marked circle. Mark a 3½-inch circle inside the

CONTINUES ON NEXT PAGE ▶

first and make indentations around this, followed by a 2½-inch circle in the center. Decorate in the same way. Mark one more circle in the center, about 1½ inches. Make three more panels in the same way.

6 Thinly roll out 9 oz of the gray icing on a counter dusted with icing sugar until large enough to cover the 10-inch cake board. Lightly dampen the board and lift the rolled icing over it. Smooth out to the edges and trim off the excess with a sharp knife. Cover the 9-inch board with 7 oz icing and the 8-inch board with 5 oz icing. Leave the boards and side panels to harden for 2 days.

7 For the buttercream, beat together the butter, confectioners' sugar, and cocoa until smooth and creamy. If the cakes have domed up in the center during baking, cut a slice off so the tops are level. To make sure the cake will be a cube shape when assembled, measure the height and width, which must be the same. If necessary, trim a little more off each cake. Cut each cake in half horizontally. Cut the centers out of two of the layers to leave a wall of cake 1¼ inches thick around the edges.

8 Spread the edges of one of the solid cake layers with a little buttercream and place a hollowed-out cake layer on top. Spread the edges of this with buttercream and position the other hollowed-out cake on top. Spread the edges of this with more buttercream. Fill the cake cavity with the chocolates and candies and position the remaining cake layer on top. Place the iced cake boards on top of one another to create steps. Transfer the cake to the top board.

9 Spread a thin layer of buttercream over the sides of the cake with a palette knife. Gently lift one panel on one hand, invert it onto the other and peel away the paper. Press the panel gently against one side of the cake so the panel sits squarely at one end with the cake, but juts out ¼ inch at the other. Position the next panel against this and then the third and fourth.

10 Spread more buttercream over the top of the cake until level with the top of the iced sides. Roll out the remaining gray icing and cut out a square to fit the top of the cake. Dampen the top edges of the side panels with water and position the top, smoothing down gently to fit. Secure a gray ribbon around the sides of the boards with double-sided tape or dressmaker's pins. If desired, spray a little black spray around the edges of the box to create an aged effect.

COOK'S TIPS

Ready-colored icing is the easiest to use and is available online and from cake decorating stores. Alternatively, you can buy white ready-to-roll icing and knead in black food coloring until the icing is dark gray. To make a professional-looking cake, you'll need perfectly measured side panels so they meet neatly at the corners. Before rolling out the side panels, measure the width of the cake. The panels should be cut to this width plus an additional ¼ inch.

HELLO, SWEETIES

FRUIT SALAD EYE STALKS

In some parts of the galaxy, people fighting the Daleks collect the eye stalks of Daleks they've destroyed as trophies. But these Dalek eye stalks are a lot easier and less dangerous to get hold of. A few apple slices, pieces of kiwifruit, and a plum threaded onto skewers make incredibly effective-looking Dalek eye stalks! Use metal kebab skewers if you have them as they're sturdier. If not, bamboo skewers will do. Serve with a bowl of honey yogurt for a fun, easy dessert.

MAKES 4 KEBABS

3–4 small red-skinned
    eating apples
2 tsp lemon or lime juice
4 round plums
4 kiwifruit
4 blueberries
3 tbsp honey
scant ½ cup Greek-style yogurt

YOU WILL NEED:
4 skewers

1 Cut the apples into thin slices, leaving the cores intact. Brush each side of the apple slices with lemon or lime juice to stop them browning.

2 Cut a thin slice off the stalk end of each plum. Use the tip of a sharp knife or an apple corer to ease out the pits, keeping the fruit intact.

3 Peel the kiwifruit and use an apple corer to cut out as many lengths of kiwi as you can from each. Cut four of the lengths into smaller ½-inch lengths.

4 Carefully thread a length of kiwi onto a skewer. Add an apple slice, then a short length of kiwi. Add three more apple slices, threading a short length of kiwi between each. Thread another long length of kiwifruit. Push a ¾-inch length of kiwi into a plum to fill the cavity. Thread the plum onto the skewer so the cut side is threaded last. You'll need a ¼-inch tip of the skewer left at the end after threading the fruit, so if necessary slide the fruits back toward the tip. Push a blueberry onto the tip. Make the remaining kebabs in the same way.

5 For the honey yogurt dip, beat the honey into the Greek-style yogurt. Serve in a bowl with the fruit kebabs.

EXTERMINATED JELLY SKELETON

If you get shot by a Dalek—and I wouldn't recommend it—then the blast from its gun is so powerful that your whole skeleton becomes visible. These piped meringues create incredibly effective "bones," making a fun dessert for a kids' party or family gathering. The meringues can be made several days in advance and stored in an airtight container. The jelly's best made up to a day ahead.

SERVES 6

2 medium egg whites
½ cup superfine sugar
3 eating apples
2 tsp lemon juice
2 tablets lime-flavored jelly
1¾ cups boiling water
lightly whipped cream, to serve

YOU WILL NEED:
a large pastry bag fitted with a
½-inch plain piping tip

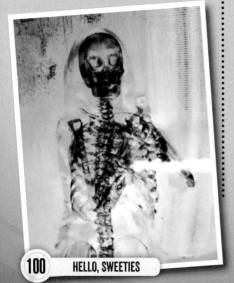

1 Preheat the oven to 250°F. Line two baking sheets with baking parchment.

2 Put the egg whites in a thoroughly clean bowl and whisk with a handheld electric whisk until softly peaking. Sprinkle in a heaping tablespoonful of the sugar and whisk for 15 seconds. Continue to whisk the mixture, adding a spoonful of sugar at a time and whisking well between each addition, until the meringue is stiff and glossy.

3 Spoon into a large pastry bag fitted with a ½-inch plain piping tip. Pipe an 3–3½-inch length of meringue onto the paper. Pipe an extra blob at each end to create a bone shape. Carry on until you have used up all the mixture. Bake for about 1 hour or until the meringues feel crisp and dry. Let cool completely on the paper.

4 For the jelly, peel, core, and finely grate the apples into a bowl and stir in the lemon juice. Separate the jelly cubes into a bowl. Add the boiling water and stir frequently until the jelly has dissolved. Pour over the grated apple, stir in 1¼ cups cold water, and leave until cool but not set. Transfer to a shallow serving dish and chill for several hours until set.

5 To serve, arrange some of the meringue bones on top of the jelly. Serve with whipped cream.

ADIPOSE PAVLOVA

The Adipose were made of people's excess body fat. But unlike the little white aliens in Doctor Who, this dessert "Adipose" is big, chubby, and completely fat-free! It's a crisp meringue on the outside with a fruity little heart. Serve with whipped cream for a delicious pavlova-style dessert.

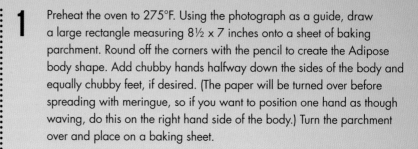

SERVES 6

4 medium egg whites
scant ¾ cup superfine sugar
scant ½ cup unrefined superfine
   sugar
2 tsp vanilla extract
1 cup mixed raspberries,
   blackberries, and blueberries
1 mini marshmallow
lightly whipped cream, to serve

COOK'S TIP

If you think the meringue might break up as you transfer it to a platter or board, cut off the surplus paper by cutting around the meringue with a scalpel, then slide onto the platter or board.

1 Preheat the oven to 275°F. Using the photograph as a guide, draw a large rectangle measuring 8½ x 7 inches onto a sheet of baking parchment. Round off the corners with the pencil to create the Adipose body shape. Add chubby hands halfway down the sides of the body and equally chubby feet, if desired. (The paper will be turned over before spreading with meringue, so if you want to position one hand as though waving, do this on the right hand side of the body.) Turn the parchment over and place on a baking sheet.

2 Whisk the egg whites in a thoroughly clean bowl until softly peaking. Combine the two sugars, add 1 tbsp to the whites and whisk for 15 seconds. Continue adding the sugar, a spoonful at a time and whisking well between each addition. Whisk in the vanilla extract with the last of the sugar.

3 Secure the baking parchment to the baking sheet by placing a blob of meringue under each corner of the paper. Spoon half the meringue into the figure and spread to the edges with a palette knife. Spread more meringue into the hand and feet areas. Set aside three of the largest blueberries. Sprinkle the remaining fruits into the center of the meringue and spoon the rest of the meringue on top. Spread to cover the fruits.

4 Using a palette knife, spread all the meringue as smoothly as you can. Make slight dips into the meringue with the back of a teaspoon where the eyes will be positioned.

5 Bake for 1½ hours or until the surface feels crisp to the touch. Let cool completely on the baking sheet. Loosen the meringue from the paper with a spatula (see Cook's tip) and carefully transfer the meringue to a large flat serving platter or board. Position two reserved blueberries for eyes. Halve the remaining blueberry and cut a slightly smiling mouth from one half. Position on the meringue and add the mini marshmallow for the single tooth. Serve with whipped cream.

DAVROS' THIRD EYE BROWNIES

Almost everything about Davros, the creator of the Daleks, has been augmented or enhanced to keep him alive. That includes his vision. His own eyes barely work anymore, so he has an electronic eye in the middle of his forehead. Scooped semicircles of fresh pear make effective, glassy-looking eyes, particularly when they're brushed with blue-colored honey! Do this just before serving for maximum impact.

MAKES 12 BROWNIES

7 oz semisweet chocolate, chopped
9 tbsp slightly salted butter
2 medium eggs
scant 1 cup light brown sugar
1 tsp vanilla extract
9 tbsp self-rising flour

TO FINISH:
2–3 large ripe pears, peeled
    and cored
1 tbsp lemon juice
3 oz milk chocolate, chopped
$^2/_3$ cup slightly salted butter
about 1 cup confectioners' sugar
3 tbsp unsweetened cocoa
1 tbsp honey
a few drops of blue food coloring

YOU WILL NEED:
a 12-cup muffin tray and a pastry
bag fitted with a ½-inch star tip

1 Preheat the oven to 350°F. Grease a 12-cup muffin tray. Put half the semisweet chocolate in a heatproof bowl with the butter and melt, either in short spurts in the microwave or by resting the bowl over a pan of gently simmering water. Stir occasionally until completely smooth.

2 Put the eggs, brown sugar, and vanilla extract in a bowl and whisk with a handheld electric whisk for 2–3 minutes until thickened and pale. Stir in the melted chocolate mixture. Sift the flour into the bowl, add the remaining chopped chocolate, and gently stir the ingredients together. Spoon into the muffin tray sections.

3 Bake for 17–20 minutes until slightly risen and a crust has formed. The cakes will still feel slightly soft. Let cool completely in the tray. Loosen the edges with a knife and lift out.

4 To shape the eyes, use a 1 tbsp measuring spoon and scoop semicircles of flesh out of the pears. Place in a bowl and coat in the lemon juice to prevent browning. (Dice the remaining fruit, toss with a little extra lemon juice and set aside for a fruit salad.) Melt the milk chocolate as above. Beat the butter and confectioners' sugar in a bowl until creamy and stir in the melted chocolate and cocoa. Place in a pastry bag fitted with a ½-inch star tip. Pipe a blob onto the center of each cake. Place a piece of pear on top and pipe some chocolate cream on either side.

5 Just before serving, mix together the honey and blue food coloring and brush over the pear eyes.

"I regret I cannot **OPEN MY** *EYES.*"

TIME ROTOR SODAS

The central column of the TARDIS control console is sometimes referred to as the Time Rotor, although the term has also been used for other controls. But it's the transparent central column that we're recreating here in edible form. The "glasses" for this fun drink are, in fact, made of colored ice. All you need to make them are two disposable plastic drinks tumblers, a drop of food coloring, and a bit of freezer space! Allow plenty of freezing time, at least overnight, so you can freeze the ice, remove from the plastic and refreeze the ice glasses, all ready for filling with a lovely minty ice-cream soda.

FOR EACH SODA

a little green or blue food coloring
2–3 scoops of mint, vanilla, or
    pistachio ice cream
chilled lemonade or cream soda

YOU WILL NEED:
inexpensive clear disposable tumblers are the best for making ice glasses. You can make any size "glass" as long as the inner tumbler is about half the capacity of the larger one. So if you have a18-oz capacity tumbler for the larger size, the smaller one should be about 9 oz

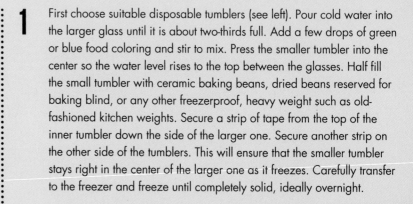

1 First choose suitable disposable tumblers (see left). Pour cold water into the larger glass until it is about two-thirds full. Add a few drops of green or blue food coloring and stir to mix. Press the smaller tumbler into the center so the water level rises to the top between the glasses. Half fill the small tumbler with ceramic baking beans, dried beans reserved for baking blind, or any other freezerproof, heavy weight such as old-fashioned kitchen weights. Secure a strip of tape from the top of the inner tumbler down the side of the larger one. Secure another strip on the other side of the tumblers. This will ensure that the smaller tumbler stays right in the center of the larger one as it freezes. Carefully transfer to the freezer and freeze until completely solid, ideally overnight.

2 Remove the weights from the small tumbler and peel away the tape. Fill the small tumbler with very hot but not boiling water, leave for 2–3 seconds, then tip out. Twist the small tumbler and ease out of the ice. If it refuses to budge, fill with hot water for another couple of seconds and try again, but take care not to melt the ice. If the ice shows any sign of melting, return it to the freezer for a couple of hours.

3 Fill a large bowl or pitcher with hot water. Dip the large tumbler into the water right up to the rim for a couple of seconds. Lift out and twist the tumbler away from the ice. If necessary, redip the tumbler. Once removed, return the ice tumbler to the freezer for at least 1 hour or until ready to serve.

4 Fill the ice tumbler with two or three scoops of ice cream. Top up with chilled lemonade or cream soda and serve.

BANANA PARTY POPS

When he first met Captain Jack, the Ninth Doctor swapped Jack's gun for a banana. He worked the same trick later, as the Eleventh Doctor, with River Song. And the Tenth Doctor imparted to Rose the immortal advice: "Always take a banana to a party ... Bananas are good." This fabulous ice cream takes the Doctor at his word and is made from one ingredient—bananas! Frozen bananas, whizzed up in a food processor, are transformed into a meltingly smooth ice cream.

MAKES 4 ICE POPS

4 small bananas
colored sugar sprinkles (optional)

YOU WILL NEED:
4 popsicle molds and 4 popsicle sticks

1 Freeze the whole bananas in their skins for 4–6 hours, or overnight.

2 Run the bananas under the tap to soften their skins. Peel away the skins or scrape off with a knife, whichever is easiest. Cut each into about six chunks and put in a food processor. Process for 1–2 minutes until smooth and creamy, scraping down any pieces from the sides of the bowl.

3 Spoon into four popsicle molds. If the mixture is still very thick, you might need to push a skewer through the mixture and stir to remove any air bubbles. Push popsicle sticks into the mixture and freeze for at least 2 hours to firm up.

4 Loosen from the molds by running them under warm water. If desired, use the sugar sprinkles to decorate one side of each ice pop with a Doctor Who symbol, such as a question mark. Serve and enjoy!

FANCY A JELLY BABY?

The Doctor has always liked jelly babies. Especially the Fourth Doctor, who often offered them round, although sometimes he said it was a jelly baby when it was some other candy. But jelly babies were certainly his preference. His favorite flavor, he once said, was orange. Homemade jelly babies taste so much fruitier and tangier than any bought ones. Strawberries and blackberries work well together both in color and flavor, though you could use the same quantity of other soft fruits like raspberries, black currants, and blueberries. Once they're shaped and set, serve them as Doctor Who would, in little paper candy bags.

MAKES 1 LB 10 OZ JELLY BABIES

2 cups blackberries
2 cups strawberries
15 leaves gelatin
1 cup superfine sugar, plus extra
   sugar for coating

YOU WILL NEED:
a jelly baby mold

1 Process the blackberries in a food processor or blender until pureed. Press through a strainer into a bowl. Rinse out the processor and puree the strawberries. Press through a strainer into a separate bowl.

2 Soak the gelatin leaves in a bowl of cold water for 5 minutes. Put the sugar in a small pan with 5 tbsp cold water and heat gently until the sugar has completely dissolved. Remove from the heat and pour into a measuring cup. Lift the softened gelatin leaves out of the water and add to the syrup. Stir briefly until dissolved. Pour half the syrup into the strawberry puree, stirring well. Pour the remainder into the blackberry puree, stirring well.

3 Carefully fill a jelly baby mold with the purees. You'll probably need to do this in batches, in which case chill the filled molds until set and leave the remainder of the fruit purees at room temperature. If the purees start to set in the cups, soften briefly in the microwave, or stand the cup in a pan of gently simmering water until softened.

4 To loosen the jellies, run the back of the mold very briefly under warm water and tip the jellies out onto a piece of baking parchment. Sprinkle with extra sugar to coat. Store in a cool place (but not the refrigerator) until ready to serve.

GALLIFROLLIPOPS

The TARDIS allows the Doctor and his companions to understand any language. But the Time Lords have their own language too. When written it is mainly composed of the swirling circular patterns and shapes seen on these chocolate lollipops. Check out your own designs online for Gallifreyan symbols if you're feeling ambitious, or copy the simplified ones in this recipe.

MAKES 8 LOLLIPOPS

7 oz milk chocolate, chopped
a handful each of semisweet, white, and milk chocolate buttons, preferably in two sizes
2 oz white chocolate, chopped
2 oz semisweet chocolate, chopped

YOU WILL NEED:
8 wooden lollipop sticks and
2 paper pastry bags

1 Line a large tray or baking sheet with baking parchment. Put the milk chocolate in a heatproof bowl and melt, either in short spurts in the microwave or by resting the bowl over a pan of gently simmering water. Stir occasionally until completely smooth. Place eight even-size spoonfuls of the melted chocolate on the paper, spacing them well apart. Spread with the back of a spoon until 2½ inches in diameter. Push a wooden lollipop stick about halfway into each circle and spread a little of the chocolate over the stick to hide it.

2 While the chocolate is still soft, position a few of the chocolate buttons on top. You can also arrange small buttons on top of larger ones, securing the smaller ones in place with a dot of the chocolate left in the bowl. Let set in a cool place.

3 Melt the white and semisweet chocolates in separate heatproof bowls as above. Transfer to paper pastry bags. Twist the top of each bag and squeeze to see whether the chocolate flows out in a thin line. If it doesn't, snip off the merest tip. Use the chocolate to pipe decorative circles, lines, and dots onto the lollipops. Leave in a cool place until the chocolate has set before carefully peeling away the paper.

HELLO, SWEETIES

"It's Old High Gallifreyan, the ancient language of the **TIME LORDS.** Not many people understand it **THESE DAYS.**"

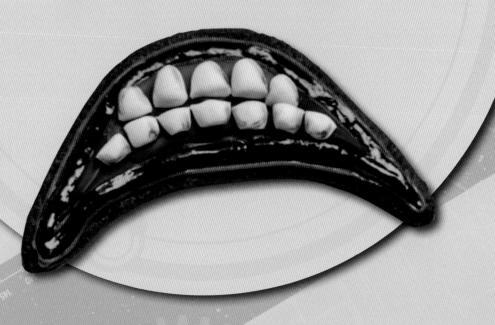

COOKIE WHO'S WHO

The Doctor's appearance may change every time he regenerates, but that just means you can create a whole set of different Doctors to serve up to your friends and family. Prepare a batch of people-shaped cookies and assemble an assortment of colored icing, tubes of writing icing, and some melted chocolate so the family can get stuck into decorating their favorite Doctor Who figure. For the shapes, trace and cut out the template (page 149) onto paper, position on the cookie dough, and cut around. Alternatively, use a gingerbread man cutter, which you can adapt by gently squeezing the limbs and bodies to slim down the shapes.

MAKES 12 COOKIES

FOR THE COOKIE DOUGH:
about 2 cups all-purpose flour, plus extra for dusting
¾ cup + 2 tbsp or 1¾ sticks firm slightly salted butter, cut into small pieces
¾ cup confectioners' sugar
2 medium egg yolks
2 tsp vanilla extract

TO DECORATE:
3 oz semisweet chocolate, chopped
3 oz milk chocolate, chopped
3 oz white chocolate, chopped
tubes of writing icing in red, blue, yellow, white, and green
2 oz each of black, red, blue, white, cream, light, and dark brown ready-to-roll icing
confectioners' sugar, for dusting

YOU WILL NEED:
a plastic food bag, 3 small paper pastry bags, or small plastic food bags, and a fine paintbrush

1 Put the flour in a food processor and add the butter. Process until the mixture resembles coarse breadcrumbs. Add the confectioners' sugar, egg yolks, and vanilla extract and process to a smooth dough. Wrap in a plastic food bag and chill for about 1 hour.

2 Preheat the oven to 375°F. Line two baking sheets with baking parchment.

3 Roll out the dough on a lightly floured counter to a ¼ inch thickness and cut out the figure shapes using the template (page 149) or a gingerbread man cutter. Space slightly apart on the baking sheets. Reroll the trimmings to make additional shapes.

4 Bake for 10–15 minutes until pale golden around the edges. Leave on the baking sheets for 2 minutes, then transfer to a wire rack to cool.

5 To decorate, melt the three chocolates separately in small heatproof bowls. Do this in the microwave in short spurts or by resting the bowls, one at a time, over a small pan of gently simmering water. Pour each melted chocolate into a small paper pastry bag and snip off the merest tip. You can also use small plastic food bags, spooning the chocolate into one corner, twisting the bag to push the chocolate into the corner, and snipping off the smallest tip. Use the three chocolates to pipe hair onto the figures.

6 For the Doctor Who clothes you can either pipe outlines of jackets, pants, coats, and sweaters onto the cookies using writing icing or thinly roll out small pieces of ready-to-roll icing on a counter dusted with confectioners' sugar and cut out the shapes. For coats and jackets, you can use the cookie cutter or template as a guide, trimming the clothes to fit once you've made the basic shape with the cutter. Secure in place with a squeeze of icing from a tube. Add accessories such as hats, umbrellas, ties, bow ties, and scarves, securing in place with a dampened fine paintbrush.

KOOKIE K-9

Built by Professor Marius, who couldn't take his real dog with him into space, K-9 was a computer made of metal and plastic. But that doesn't taste nearly as nice as gingerbread! This creation takes time and a little patience, but is worth the effort—particularly if you put a little battery-powered tealight to light up his eyes. Trace the templates on page 146–8 and cut out before you start. Once assembled, K-9 will keep, loosely covered with plastic wrap, for two days before the boiled candies start to soften.

SERVES 16

2²⁄₃ cups all-purpose flour, plus extra for dusting
2 tsp baking powder
2 tsp ground ginger
1 tsp ground mixed spice
7 tbsp firm slightly salted butter, cut into small pieces
¾ cup light brown sugar
3 tbsp light corn syrup
1 medium egg
1 medium egg yolk
1 clear red boiled candy

TO FINISH:

2 ready-made ginger loaf cakes
7 oz milk chocolate, broken into pieces
3 marshmallows
2 pieces of dried fruit slices
1-oz piece of red ready-to-roll icing
confectioners' sugar, for dusting
1 clear green boiled candy
tubes of black and green writing icing
9 small sugar-coated candies

YOU WILL NEED:

a paper pastry bag or small plastic food bag and two 8-inch cake pop sticks (cut down to size with scissors if necessary)

1 Put the flour, baking powder, ginger, and mixed spice in a food processor. Add the butter and process until the mixture resembles fine breadcrumbs. Add the sugar, syrup, egg, and egg yolk and process to a dough. Turn out onto a lightly floured counter and shape into a neat block. Wrap in plastic wrap and chill for at least 30 minutes to firm up.

2 Preheat the oven to 400°F. Line two baking sheets with baking parchment. Roll out half the dough on a lightly floured counter to a ¹⁄₈ in thickness. Transfer to a baking sheet. Place one of the largest templates over the dough and cut around with a knife. Cut out as many more templates as you can fit over the rest of the rolled dough. Lift away the excess dough and set aside. If any of the cut out pieces are very close to each other, separate them slightly, but make sure you don't distort the shapes. Roll out the remaining dough and cut out more shapes, remembering that you'll need two of some of the shapes as indicated on the templates. Re-roll the trimmings if necessary until you've cut them all out. Using a skewer, make two large holes, each about ½ inch across, into the "body top" panel as shown on the template. For K-9's eyes, cut a rectangle out of the center of the "head top eyes" panel so you're left with a small frame.

3 Bake all the sections of the gingerbread apart from the "head top eyes" panel for about 12–15 minutes until turning golden around the edges. If the holes in the "body top" have closed up, enlarge them with a skewer before the gingerbread cools. Leave on the baking sheets for 5 minutes, then transfer to a wire rack to cool. For the "head top eyes" panel, bake the frame, on baking parchment, for 5 minutes. Crush the red boiled candy into several pieces and put in the center of the frame. Return to the oven for another 5 minutes or until the candy has melted to fill the frame. Let set on the paper.

CONTINUES ON NEXT PAGE ▶

COOK'S TIP

Position a small battery-powered light behind the eye before positioning the head over the body. If it doesn't stay in place, secure it by wedging in an extra piece of marshmallow or ready-to-roll icing. Take care that you don't break the frame!

4 To assemble K-9, choose a flat board or plate for serving and stack the gingerbread cakes, one on top of another, on the center. Put the chocolate in a heatproof bowl and rest the bowl over a small pan of gently simmering water, making sure the bottom of the bowl is not in contact with the water. Turn off the heat and leave until the chocolate has melted. Alternatively, melt the chocolate in short spurts on medium power in the microwave. Spoon half the melted chocolate into a paper pastry bag or the corner of a small plastic food bag and snip off the merest tip.

5 You'll need to cut sloping sides off the top layer of ginger cake so the gingerbread pieces can rest against it for support. To get an idea of how much you'll need to cut away, lean the side and end sections of K-9 against the gingerbread. Take sloping slices off the long sides of the ginger cake so the gingerbread pieces all meet down the sides with a rectangle at the top where the body top gingerbread will fit. (You might need an extra pair of hands to do this!) Lift the gingerbread away, spread a little melted chocolate from the bowl onto the sloping sides of the ginger cake and reposition the gingerbread sides and ends. Pipe more chocolate along the joins and around the top edges. Position the body top. Chill for about 30 minutes so the chocolate firms up.

6 Meanwhile, work on a separate board and secure the head side and end pieces together as shown in the photograph. Do this by piping lines of chocolate where the sections join together. Again you might need an extra pair of hands here, or you can prop up the sections with small jars or cartons. Let set.

7 Push the cake pop sticks vertically down through the holes in the gingerbread. Push a marshmallow down over each stick so they rest on the gingerbread. Position the third marshmallow betwen the two sticks. This will help support the head. Continue assembling the head by adding the snout, eye, and top sections. Pipe lines of chocolate across the eyes. Secure the fruit slices to the head with more chocolate for ears.

8 For the collar, roll out the red icing on a counter dusted with confectioners' sugar to a long, thin strip. Cut out a 10 x ¾-inch length and drape around the neck, pressing the ends together at the front. Secure the green boiled candy over the ends of the collar with more chocolate. Pipe lines of writing icing over the collar to decorate. For the control panel, pipe a rectangle of chocolate on the top of the body and secure rows of colored candies. Pipe further rectangles of chocolate on the body sides. Once you're sure the head has completely set, carefully rest it over the head support so it tilts forward. Store in a cool place.

THE TARDIS

The world's most famous police call box is, in this case, made of cake in the center and a cookie frame. It's specially designed so that the roof lifts off for positioning a battery-powered light behind the windows. This cake is another great bake-ahead party centerpiece. You can make the entire cake, except for the window panes, three days in advance, then add the window panes a day or two before serving as they're liable to soften if left for longer. Cover loosely with plastic wrap and keep it somewhere cool and away from inquisitive fingers!

SERVES 12–15

FOR THE CAKE:

1 cup or 2 sticks slightly salted butter, softened
1¼ cups superfine sugar
2 tsp vanilla extract
4 medium eggs
about 2¼ cups self-rising flour
3 tbsp milk

FOR THE COOKIE DOUGH:

2⅔ cups all-purpose flour
1 tsp baking powder
2 tsp ground cinnamon
7 tbsp firm slightly salted butter, cut into small pieces
¾ cup light brown sugar
2 tbsp blackstrap molasses
1 medium egg
1 medium egg yolk
8 clear orange-colored boiled candies

TO DECORATE:

2½ cups confectioners' sugar
1 medium egg white
navy blue and black liquid food coloring
14 oz navy blue ready-to-roll icing
small bit each of orange and white ready-to-roll icing
7 tbsp butter, softened

YOU WILL NEED:

an 8-inch square cake pan, 2 paper pastry bags each fitted with a fine writing tip, a fine paintbrush, an 8–9-inch square silver cake board, 1 paper pastry bag fitted with a large writing tip, or a fine star tip, and a battery-powered tealight

1 Preheat the oven to 325°F. Grease and line the bottom and sides of an 8-inch square cake pan. Grease the lining paper.

2 For the cake, put the butter, superfine sugar, vanilla extract, eggs, flour, and milk in a bowl and beat with a handheld electric whisk until pale and creamy. Turn into the pan, level the surface, and bake for about 45 minutes or until just firm to the touch and a skewer inserted into the center comes out clean. Turn out onto a wire rack and let cool.

3 For the cookie dough, trace the TARDIS template (page 150) onto paper and cut out. Put the flour, baking powder, and cinnamon in a food processor. Add the butter and process until the mixture resembles fine breadcrumbs. Briefly blend in the brown sugar. Add the molasses, egg, and egg yolk and process to a paste.

4 Increase the oven temperature to 400°F. Line two baking sheets with baking parchment. Divide the dough in half and roll out each half to a ⅛ inch thickness. Transfer to the baking sheets and chill for 30 minutes.

CONTINUES ON NEXT PAGE ▶

5 Lay the TARDIS template on the dough and cut out four sections, not forgetting to cut out the windows from each. Reroll the trimmings if necessary and cut out one 5-inch square, one 3½-inch square, and one 2½-inch square. These will form the roof. Bake the cookies or 15–17 minutes or until they look cooked and are slightly darker around the edges. Let cool completely on the baking sheets.

6 Beat 1½ cups of the confectioners' sugar with the egg white until smooth. Transfer a quarter to a small bowl and keep tightly covered with plastic wrap to prevent a crust forming. Beat navy blue food coloring into the remainder to color it deep blue. Keep this tightly covered.

7 Trim ⅛-inch off all the sides of the TARDIS template (you might need to cut out another one if the original has become greasy or you'll mark the icing). Thinly roll out the blue ready-to-roll icing on a counter dusted with confectioners' sugar and cut around the TARDIS template. Dot a little of the blue icing from the bowl over one TARDIS cookie (you only need the merest scrape) and position the rolled-out blue icing on top. Repeat on the remaining three cookies.

8 Use more of the blue ready-to-roll icing to cover the cookie squares so you have a thin border of cookie left around the edge of each square. Stack these together to shape the roof. Shape a small piece of orange icing for the roof light and secure to the top of the roof with a dot of icing.

9 Put the white icing from the bowl into a small pastry bag fitted with a fine writing tip. Use to pipe POLICE PUBLIC CALL BOX at the top of one TARDIS side. Put half the blue icing in another pastry bag fitted with a fine writing tip and pipe six square panels onto each side. Shape and position a small rectangular notice to one side and a small white door handle using the white ready to roll icing. Write the notice in black food coloring using a fine paintbrush. Let dry out overnight.

POLICE

POLICE TELEPHONE
FREE
FOR USE OF
PUBLIC
ADVICE & ASSISTANCE
OBTAINABLE IMMEDIATELY
OFFICERS & CARS
RESPOND TO ALL CALLS
PULL TO OPEN

BOX

10 To assemble the TARDIS, beat together the butter and remaining confectioners' sugar until pale and creamy. Slice off any domed crust from the cake and cut the cake accurately into quarters i.e. four squares (you'll only need three pieces so the remaining piece can be eaten or frozen for another time). Sandwich the three cakes on the center of a 8–9-inch square silver cake board with half the buttercream. The assembled cake must be no taller than 5 inches. If necessary, slice a little off the top. Spread the remaining buttercream around the sides of the cake. Carefully secure the TARDIS panels to the sides of the cake, pressing them gently into position.

11 Put the remaining blue icing in a pastry bag fitted with a large writing tip (or a fine star tip). Use to pipe lines of icing down the sides of the TARDIS where the panels meet. This will seal any gaps and will set to hold the TARDIS in place.

12 To finish the windows, preheat the oven to 400°F. Line a baking sheet with baking parchment. Draw four 3½ x 2-inch rectangles onto the parchment, turn the paper over, and position two orange candies in the center of each. Bake for 5 minutes or until the candies have melted to fill the rectangles (you might need to tweak the melted candies into the corners of the squares. Don't worry if they run over the edges). Let the rectangles harden for about 15 minutes until brittle. Pipe dots of blue icing around the rim inside one of the TARDIS windows. Carefully lift one of the candy panels off the paper and press gently onto the icing to hold the window in place. Repeat on the other three sides. Pipe blue icing window panes onto the outside of the windows and around the roof light.

13 Rest a battery-powered tealight on top of the sponge cake ready for switching on, then carefully rest the roof on top.

COOK'S TIPS

This is quite a fiddly and time-consuming bake, but looks stunning and is so rewarding to make, particularly if you light it up! Take extra care when shaping and baking the TARDIS panels. If they're wonky or irregular the cake will be difficult to assemble and more likely to break. For accurate piping it's also worth buying metal writing tips in two sizes. One for the white writing and side panels and a larger one or fine star tip for piping the windows and corners. Both can be achieved by using a disposable bag and cutting off the tip, but a tip gives more professional results. To serve the cake, sprinkle crushed Graham crackers around the bottom to resemble desert, dried shredded coconut for an Arctic setting, green-colored dried shredded coconut for grass, or blue-colored sugar for "space."

SHORTBREAD SMILERS

The Smilers were the information system on Starship UK. They were happy-looking figures inside booths. But they could turn nasty in a moment. Bake the chocolate shapes for these angry mouth cookies and give the family free rein to decorate them with chocolate, jammy lips, and icing teeth. And if you want to make your Smiler nasty, simply turn the smile upside-down.

MAKES 12 COOKIES

FOR THE COOKIE DOUGH:
scant 1 cup all-purpose flour
¼ cup unsweetened cocoa
7 tbsp firm slightly salted butter, cut into pieces
scant ⅓ cup light brown sugar
1 medium egg yolk

TO DECORATE:
3 oz milk chocolate, chopped
3 oz semisweet chocolate, chopped
tube of red writing icing
2 oz ivory ready-to-roll icing
brown food coloring
6 tbsp reduced-sugar strawberry jam

YOU WILL NEED:
a paintbrush and a paper pastry bag or a plastic food bag

1 Put the flour and cocoa in a food processor and add the butter. Process until the mixture has the consistency of fine breadcrumbs. Add the sugar and egg yolk and process to a smooth dough. Turn out onto the counter and knead into a neat block. Wrap and chill for 30 minutes.

2 Preheat the oven to 375°F. Trace and cut out the Smiler template (page 151) onto paper. Grease a large baking sheet. Roll out the dough on a lightly floured counter to a ⅛ inch thickness. Place the template over the dough and cut around with a knife. Transfer to the baking sheet and cut out the remaining dough in the same way. Reroll the trimmings to make more cookies. Bake for 15 minutes. Leave on the baking sheet for 5 minutes, then transfer to a wire rack to cool.

3 Put the milk chocolate in a heatproof bowl and rest the bowl over a small pan of gently simmering water, making sure the bottom of the bowl is not in contact with the water. Turn off the heat and leave until the chocolate has melted. Alternatively, melt the chocolate in short spurts on medium power in the microwave. Do the same with the semisweet chocolate.

4 Use the red writing icing to pipe the outline of lips around the edges of the cookies. Spoon a little semisweet chocolate into the corners of each mouth and a little milk chocolate into the center. Spread the two chocolate flavors together and to the edges of the red piping with the tip of a toothpick.

5 For the teeth, take a piece of the ivory icing and roll under the palms of your hands to a ¼ inch thickness. Cut into short tooth-size lengths and arrange over the chocolate. Shape the tops of the teeth into curved shapes so they look more realistic. Cut and position shorter lengths for the lower teeth. Dilute a little brown food coloring with water to give a thin paint consistency and use to paint over the edges of the teeth using a paintbrush.

6 Press the jam through a strainer with the back of a spoon. Put the strained jam in a paper pastry bag or into one corner of a plastic food bag. Snip off the merest tip and pipe the jam into the lip area of the cookies.

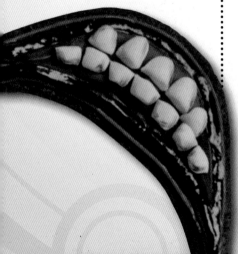

"The **SMILING** fellows in the booths. They're **EVERY-WHERE.**"

JAMMY DODGERS

Jammy Dodgers are Doctor Who's favorite cookie. Quite apart from eating them—and they do taste delicious—he used a Jammy Dodger to bluff the Daleks by pretending it was a TARDIS self-destruct button. Our version won't explode either, and they are decorated with his famous question mark motif rather than the usual heart shape, though do this if you prefer. If you're planning a Doctor Who party, make these a day in advance and store in an airtight container.

MAKES 16 COOKIES

1½ cups all-purpose flour, plus extra for dusting
½ cup cornstarch
¾ cup + 1 tsp or 1½ sticks firm unsalted butter, cut into small pieces
scant ½ cup superfine sugar
1 tsp vanilla extract

TO FINISH:
¾ cup confectioners' sugar
5 tbsp unsalted butter, softened
4–5 tbsp strawberry jam

YOU WILL NEED:
a 2½-inch plain round cutter and a question mark cookie cutter, or a fine scalpel

1 Put the flour and cornstarch in a food processor and add the butter. Process until the mixture resembles coarse breadcrumbs. Add the superfine sugar and vanilla and process to a firm dough. Turn out onto a lightly floured counter and knead into a block. Wrap and chill for 1 hour.

2 Preheat the oven to 375°F. Grease two baking sheets. Roll out the dough to a ⅛ inch thickness and cut out circles using a 2½-inch plain cutter. Transfer to the baking sheet and reroll the trimmings to make extra. You should have enough dough to make 32 circles.

3 Using a question mark cookie cutter, cut out the shape from half the circles. Alternatively, cut out the shapes freehand using a fine scalpel.

4 Bake for 12–15 minutes or until pale golden. If the question mark shapes have closed up a little during baking, open them out with the tip of a knife while still warm. Leave on the baking sheets for 5 minutes, then transfer to a wire rack to cool.

5 To finish, beat together the confectioners' sugar and butter until smooth. Spread over the plain cookie halves and spoon a little jam on top. Position the lids. Store in an airtight container.

CAPTAIN FLAPJACKS

Captain Jack Harkness, Torchwood agent and sometime companion to the Tenth Doctor, is an immortal—but these tasty little treats won't last nearly so long. With chunks of cookie, nuts, seeds, and dried fruit, all coated in a thick layer of white chocolate, they are just as seductive as Jack himself. Or just great for a family tea or lunchbox filler.

MAKES 12 FLAPJACKS

3 oz Graham crackers or oat cookies

$1/3$ cup almonds, finely chopped

$1/4$ cup golden raisins

$1/3$ cup dried apricots or pitted dates, chopped

4 tbsp sunflower or pumpkin seeds

11 oz white chocolate, chopped

3 tbsp butter

YOU WILL NEED:

a shallow 7-inch square pan (if you don't have this pan size, use a similar-size container such as a plastic food box)

1 Line the bottom and sides of a shallow 7-inch square cake pan with plastic wrap that overhangs the sides of the pan. Crumble the cookies into a bowl and stir in the almonds, golden raisins, apricots or dates, and seeds.

2 Put 7 oz of the white chocolate in a heatproof bowl with the butter and melt, either in short spurts in the microwave or by resting the bowl over a pan of gently simmering water. Stir occasionally until completely smooth. Add to the dry ingredients and mix well. Turn into the pan and pack down firmly with the back of a dessertspoon until compact and level. Bring the edges of the plastic wrap over the filling and press down to compact the ingredients further.

3 Melt the remaining white chocolate as above and spread over the surface of the filling. Chill for 1–2 hours until firm.

4 Transfer the slab to a board and peel away the plastic wrap. Cut in half, then across into bars. Store in an airtight container.

JUDOON CREAM HORNS

The Judoon are a mercenary police force. They look rather like upright rhinoceroses—complete with horns. Though if you tried to get hold of a Judoon horn, you'd probably be executed on the spot for assault. Serving chocolate mousse in ice-cream cones is a fun idea for a kids' party and saves you having to serve on plates! If possible use waffle cones as opposed to the wafer ones.

MAKES 10 CREAM HORNS

6 oz semisweet chocolate, chopped
10 ice-cream cones
3 oz milk chocolate, chopped
4 tbsp heavy cream
4 medium egg whites
1 tbsp superfine sugar
chocolate flavor sprinkles
unsweetened cocoa, for dusting

1 Put 3½ oz of the semisweet chocolate in a heatproof bowl and rest the bowl over a pan of gently simmering water, making sure the bottom of the bowl is not in contact with the water. Turn off the heat and leave until the chocolate has melted. Spoon a little of the melted chocolate into an ice-cream cone and spread up the sides with a pastry brush. Repeat with the remainder and chill while making the mousse.

2 Put the remaining semisweet chocolate, the milk chocolate, and cream in the bowl and melt over the heat again as before. Stir occasionally until smooth.

3 Whisk the egg whites in a thoroughly clean bowl until only just peaking. When the whisk is lifted from the bowl, the peaks should just start to flop over. Whisk in the sugar. Using a large metal spoon, fold a quarter of the whites into the chocolate mixture. Scrape the chocolate mixture out into the remaining whites and fold gently together until no streaks of egg white remain.

4 Place the ice-cream cones in tumblers ready for filling. Half fill each cone with mousse, then tap the tumblers on the surface to make sure the mousse sinks down to the bottom. Fill each cone to the top. Sprinkle the chocolate flavor sprinkles on top and return to the refrigerator for several hours until firm.

5 Invert the cones onto a serving platter and dust with cocoa.

EXTERMINATE-A-CAKE POPS

Although the Daleks themselves are unlikely to invent edible components for their casings, or make their sucker arms and guns into tasty snacks, you can do it for them. Just don't let them find out—or you might get a taste of real extermination. These little cakey treats are fun to make and require no baking. Just allow plenty of time for chilling them after shaping, so they're firm enough to coat in chocolate and finish decorating.

MAKES 12 CAKE POPS

11½ oz bought or homemade
    Madeira cake
8 oz white chocolate, chopped
3 tbsp heavy cream

TO DECORATE:
5 oz semisweet chocolate,
    chopped
5 oz white chocolate, chopped
tubes of black and white writing
    icing
silver food coloring

YOU WILL NEED:
12 cake pop sticks and a fine
paintbrush

1 Line a tray or baking sheet with baking parchment. Finely crumble the cake into a bowl. Put the white chocolate in a heatproof bowl and melt, either in short spurts in the microwave or by resting the bowl over a pan of gently simmering water. Add the melted chocolate to the cake crumbs with the cream. Stir well to make a thick, evenly mixed paste.

2 For the Dalek suckers, take 3 oz of the mixture and press in the palms of your hands into a firm, round ball. Cut in half and place each half, flat-side face down, on the paper. Press a cake pop stick down through the center of each one. Gently push the mixture around the sticks so it remains upright. Shape four more suckers (from two more balls) in the same way.

3 For the Dalek gun sticks, take a 1½-oz piece of the mixture and shape into a thick sausage, about 3½ inches long. Push a cake pop stick in one end and through about two-thirds of the mixture. Make five more in the same way. Place on the paper and chill all the cake pops for several hours until firm.

4 To finish, melt the semisweet and white chocolates in separate heatproof bowls as above. Line the tray with clean baking parchment. Dip one of the suckers in the melted semisweet chocolate until coated, letting the excess chocolate drip back into the bowl. Transfer to the clean paper and coat the remainder in the same way. Coat the gun sticks in the melted white chocolate. Chill the pops for 20–30 minutes until the chocolate is firm.

5 Pipe two bands of black writing icing around the Dalek sucker cake pops where the chocolate meets the stick. Holding one of the Dalek gun sticks, vertically pipe lines of white writing icing, ½ inch apart, down the length of the chocolate coating. As you finish each one, push the stick into a bowl filled with superfine sugar to support the cake pop as it dries. Repeat with the remainder. Let set.

6 Using a fine paintbrush, paint the white writing icing with silver food coloring.

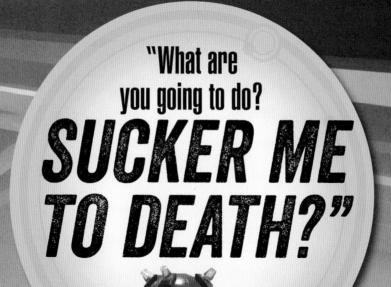

"What are you going to do?
SUCKER ME TO DEATH?"

TIMEY-WIMEY TEMPLATES

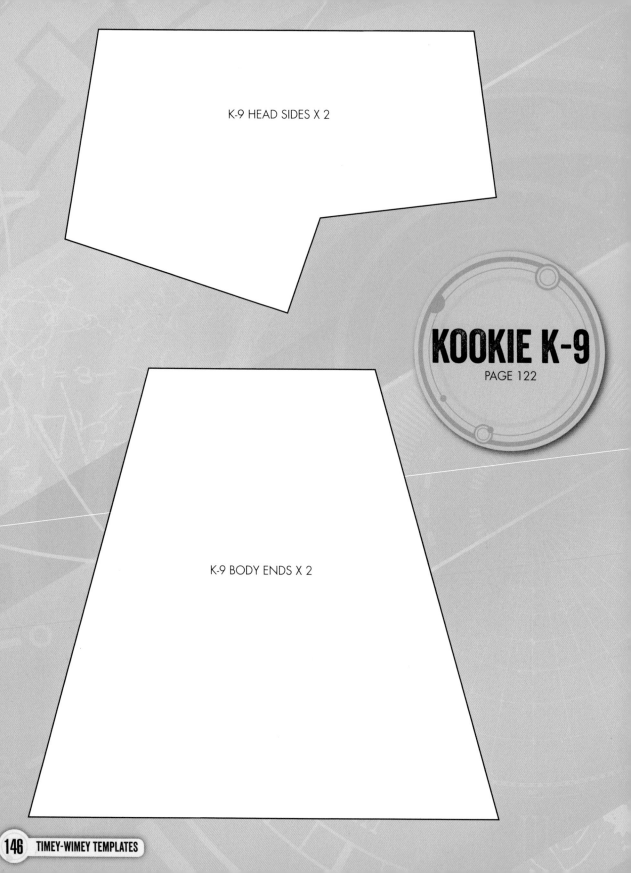

K-9 HEAD SIDES X 2

KOOKIE K-9
PAGE 122

K-9 BODY ENDS X 2

K-9 BODY SIDES X 2

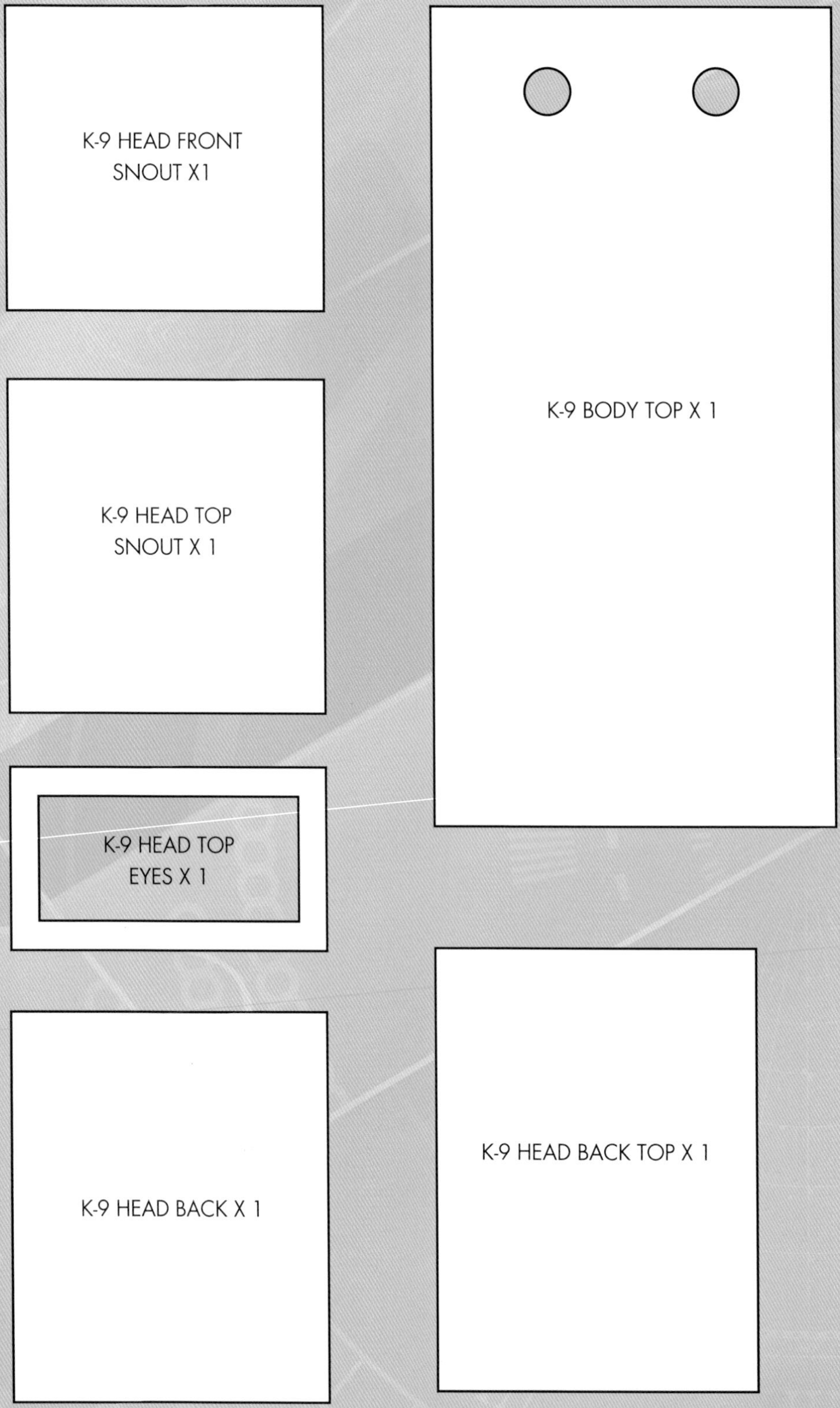

K-9 HEAD FRONT
SNOUT X1

K-9 BODY TOP X 1

K-9 HEAD TOP
SNOUT X 1

K-9 HEAD TOP
EYES X 1

K-9 HEAD BACK X 1

K-9 HEAD BACK TOP X 1

COOKIE
WHO'S
WHO
PAGE 120

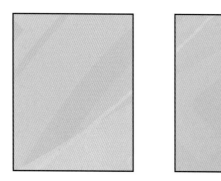

THE TARDIS
PAGE 126

TARDIS X 4

CHRISTMAS SNOWMAN
PAGE 88

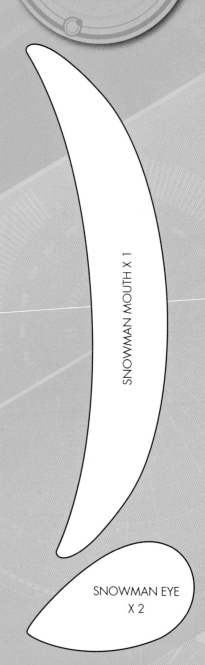

SNOWMAN MOUTH X 1

SNOWMAN EYE
X 2

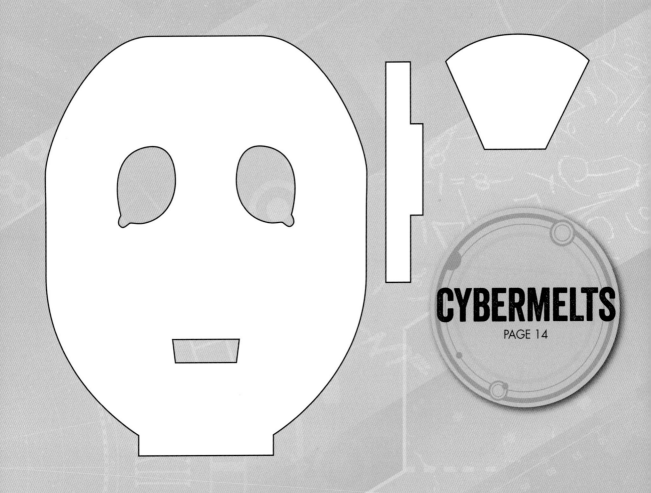

CYBERMELTS
PAGE 14

SHORTBREAD SMILERS
PAGE 130

SMILER MOUTH

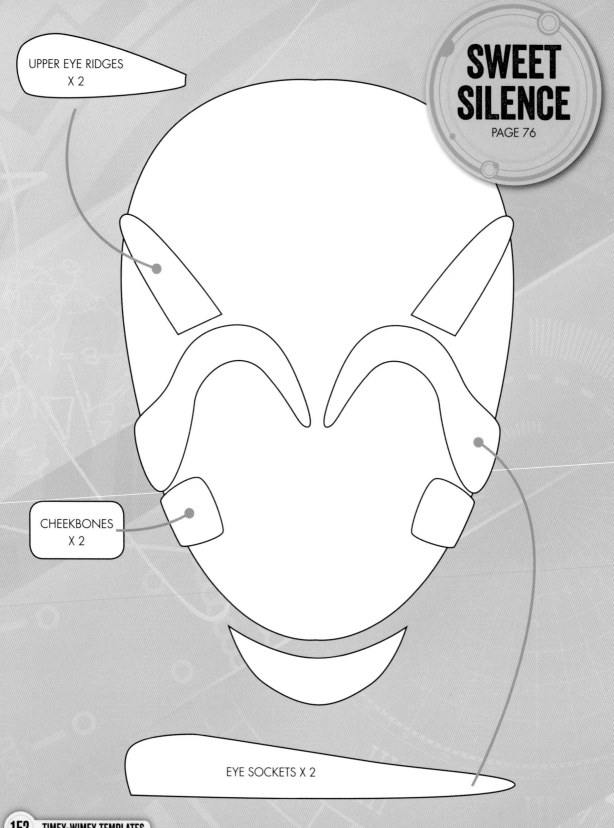

UPPER EYE RIDGES
X 2

SWEET
SILENCE
PAGE 76

CHEEKBONES
X 2

EYE SOCKETS X 2

HEAD

INDEX

First published in 2016 by
Harper Design
An Imprint of HarperCollins*Publishers*
195 Broadway
New York, NY 10007
Tel: (212) 207-7000
Fax: 855-746-6023
harperdesign@harpercollins.com
www.hc.com

This edition distributed throughout the world by:
HarperCollins*Publishers*
195 Broadway
New York, NY 10007

Library of Congress Control Number: 2016932673

ISBN 978-0-06-245562-8

First Printing, 2016

Editorial Director: Albert DePetrillo
Commissioning Editor: Kate Fox
Series Consultant: Justin Richards
Copyeditor: Kay Delves
Design: Amazing15
Photography and Prop Styling: Haarala Hamilton
Production: Phil Spencer and Alex Goddard

Color origination by BORN Ltd
Printed and bound in China by Toppan Leefung